First World War
and Army of Occupation
War Diary
France, Belgium and Germany

47 DIVISION
Divisional Troops
237 Brigade Royal Field Artillery
1 March 1915 - 29 November 1916

WO95/2717/5

The Naval & Military Press Ltd
www.nmarchive.com
Published in association with The National Archives

Published by

The Naval & Military Press Ltd

Unit 10 Ridgewood Industrial Park,

Uckfield, East Sussex,

TN22 5QE England

Tel: +44 (0) 1825 749494

www.naval-military-press.com

www.nmarchive.com

This diary has been reprinted in facsimile from the original. Any imperfections are inevitably reproduced and the quality may fall short of modern type and cartographic standards.

© **Crown Copyright**
Images reproduced by permission of The National Archives, London, England, 2015.

Contents

Document type	Place/Title	Date From	Date To
Heading	WO95/2717 Mar 1915-Nov 1916 237 Brigade Royal Field Artillery		
Heading	47th Division 1-7th London Brigade R.F.A. Became 237th Brigade R.F.A. Mar 1915-Nov 1916		
Heading	2nd London Divn 1/7th London Bde RFA Vol I 1-31.3.15		
War Diary	Bosemoor	01/03/1915	17/03/1915
War Diary	Gavre	18/03/1915	18/03/1915
War Diary	France	19/03/1915	31/03/1915
Heading	2nd London Division 7th London Brigade RFA Vol II 1-28.4.15		
War Diary	Auchel	01/04/1915	10/04/1915
War Diary	Cambrin	11/04/1915	28/04/1915
Heading	47th Division 7th London Bde R.F.A. Vol III 1-31.5.15		
War Diary	Cambrin	01/05/1915	31/05/1915
Heading	47th Division 7th London Bde R.F.A. Vol IV 1-30.6.15		
War Diary	Noyelles	01/06/1915	07/06/1915
War Diary	Ames	08/06/1915	23/06/1915
War Diary	Lapugnoy	24/06/1915	30/06/1915
Heading	47th Division 1/7th London Bde R.F.A. Vol V From 1st To 31st July 1915		
War Diary	Pugnoy	01/07/1918	08/07/1918
War Diary	Grenay	09/07/1918	29/07/1918
War Diary	Gosnay	30/07/1918	31/07/1918
Heading	47th Division 1/7th London Bde RFA Vol VI August 15		
War Diary	Gosnay	01/08/1915	10/08/1915
War Diary	Lozinghem	12/08/1915	31/08/1915
Miscellaneous	Weekly Strength Return	06/08/1915	06/08/1915
Miscellaneous	Weekly Strength Return	13/08/1915	13/08/1915
Miscellaneous	Weekly Strength Return	19/08/1915	19/08/1915
Miscellaneous	Weekly Strength Return	26/08/1915	26/08/1915
Heading	War Diary Headquarters 237th Brigade R.F.A. (1/7 London) (47th Division) September 1915		
War Diary	Lozinghem	01/09/1915	01/09/1915
War Diary	Bois Des Dames	02/09/1915	21/09/1915
War Diary	Haillicourt	22/09/1915	30/09/1915
Heading	Weekly Strength Returns		
Miscellaneous	Weekly Strength Returns Of 7th London Brigade RFA	02/09/1915	02/09/1915
Miscellaneous	Weekly Strength Returns Of 7th London Brigade RFA	09/09/1915	09/09/1915
Miscellaneous	Weekly Strength Returns Of 7th London Brigade RFA	16/09/1915	16/09/1915
Miscellaneous	Weekly Strength Returns Of 7th London Brigade RFA	23/09/1915	23/09/1915
Miscellaneous	Weekly Strength Returns Of 7th London Brigade RFA	30/09/1915	30/09/1915
Heading	47th Division 7th London Bde R.F.A. Vol VIII Oct 15		
War Diary	Lesbrebis	01/10/1915	01/10/1915
War Diary	Hesdigneul	02/10/1915	03/10/1915
War Diary	Labeuvriere	04/10/1915	06/10/1915
War Diary	Marles	07/10/1915	15/10/1915
War Diary	Philosophe	16/10/1915	31/10/1915

Heading	47th Division 1/7th London Bde R.F.A. Nov 1915 Vol IX		
War Diary	Vermelles	01/11/1915	16/11/1915
War Diary	Cauchy A-La-Tour	17/11/1915	30/11/1915
Heading	47th 7th London Bde R.F.A. Dec Vol X		
War Diary	Rincq	01/12/1915	01/12/1915
War Diary	Cauchy A La Tour	02/12/1915	15/12/1915
War Diary	Sailly La Bourse	16/12/1915	31/12/1915
Heading	1/7 London Bde RFA Jan Vol XI		
War Diary	Sailly-La-Bourse	04/01/1916	05/01/1916
War Diary	Les Brebis	06/01/1916	31/01/1916
Heading	1/7 London Bde R.F.A. Feb Vol XII		
War Diary	Les Brebis	01/02/1916	16/02/1916
War Diary	Mazingarbe	17/02/1916	29/02/1916
Heading	1/7 London Bde R.F.A. Vol XIII		
War Diary	Camblain	12/03/1916	12/03/1916
War Diary	Chatelain	13/03/1916	18/03/1916
War Diary	Bois De Bouvigny	19/03/1916	19/03/1916
War Diary	X2 B.55 Map Sheet 36 C S.E 1/20,000	20/03/1916	26/03/1916
War Diary	Bois De Bouvigny	28/03/1916	10/04/1916
War Diary	Frevillers	12/04/1916	17/04/1916
War Diary	Bois De Bouvigny	18/04/1916	30/04/1916
War Diary	Le Conte	01/05/1916	19/05/1916
War Diary	Bois de la Haye	20/05/1916	22/05/1916
War Diary	Berthonval	22/05/1916	26/05/1916
War Diary	Brias	27/05/1916	31/05/1916
War Diary	Barlin	02/06/1916	30/06/1916
Heading	47th Divisional Artillery 237th Brigade Royal Field Artillery July 1916		
War Diary	Barlin	01/07/1916	08/07/1916
War Diary	Aix Noulette	09/07/1916	28/07/1916
War Diary	Gricourt	29/07/1916	30/07/1916
War Diary	Monchel	30/07/1916	31/07/1916
Heading	47th Divisional Artillery 237th Brigade Royal Field Artillery August 1916		
War Diary	Wavans	01/08/1916	04/08/1916
War Diary	Le Ponchel	05/08/1916	09/08/1916
War Diary	Lanches	10/08/1916	10/08/1916
War Diary	Naours	11/08/1916	11/08/1916
War Diary	Behencourt	12/08/1916	13/08/1916
War Diary	Mametz	14/08/1916	15/09/1916
War Diary	High Wood	16/09/1916	22/09/1916
War Diary	Mametz	23/09/1916	07/10/1916
War Diary	Eaucourt L'Abbaye	08/10/1916	13/10/1916
War Diary	Pierregot	14/10/1916	15/10/1916
War Diary	Amplier	16/10/1916	16/10/1916
War Diary	Ligny-Sur-Canche	17/10/1916	17/10/1916
War Diary	Heuchin	18/10/1916	18/10/1916
War Diary	Rebecqe	19/10/1916	19/10/1916
War Diary	Abeele	20/10/1916	22/10/1916
War Diary	Ypres	01/11/1916	29/11/1916

(5) WO95/2717

Mar 1915 – Nov 1916

237 Brigade Royal Field Artillery

47TH DIVISION

1-7TH LONDON BRIGADE R.F.A.
BECAME:
237TH BRIGADE R.F.A.
MAR 1915-NOV 1916

Bde Broken up

121/48/4

2nd London Divn

1/7th London Bde. R.F.A.

Vol I. 1 – 31. 3. 15.

WAR DIARY or INTELLIGENCE SUMMARY

Army Form C. 2118.

Instructions regarding War Diaries and Intelligence Summaries are contained in F.S. Regs., Part II. and the Staff Manual respectively. Title pages will be prepared in manuscript.

1/4th London Regt. R.F.A.

March 1915

Place	Date	Hour	Summary of Events and Information	Remarks and references to Appendices
Bournemouth	1/3/15		Col. Chambers to France for 3 days attachment	
"	3/3/15		Horse Inspection by Major Bankes	
"	4/3/15		Horse Inspection by A.D.V.S. 3rd Army	
"	5/3/15		Instructions received from W.O. & and Telephone Rent to 3rd London Bde R.F.A.	
"	6/3/15		Col. Chambers returned from France	
"	10/3/15		Enquiry at Bemis Templeton, Iron Bark, re sale of oats and exchange of ration	
"	11/3/15	5 p.m.	Instructions recd for Officer to select billets at Barnsbury Park, Watford	
"	12/3/15		Brigade moved to Barnsbury Park. Disinfection of men, horses, harness etc	
"	13/3/15		Disinfection continued	
"	14/3/15		Brigade made up to War Strength in Horses from 3rd London Reserve Brigade R.F.A.	
"	15/3/15		Ordnance Stores received. Horses Saved, harness fitted	
"	16/3/15		Ditto	
"	17/3/15			
France	18/3/15		Brigade railed to Southam (Am Entrained Southam fitted) Comdt to Same	
"			Arrived Same 11 a.m. Detrained. Went to No 2 Rest Camp, Same	
France	19/3/15		Brigade railed to Argues. Billeted there for the night on 20th	
"	20/3/15		Brigade arrived at Argues. Reset train 3 p.m. Billeted there for night	

WAR DIARY
or
INTELLIGENCE SUMMARY.
(Erase heading not required.)

Army Form C. 2118.

Place	Date	Hour	Summary of Events and Information	Remarks and references to Appendices
France	21/3		Brigade marched to AUCHEL, arriving there 4 p.m. 25 mile march	
	22/3		Division inspected by Sir John French	
	28/3		Lecture by Gen. Montgomery	
	24/3		Major Mead, Lonec. Mangat & Capt. Lloyd attached to 31st Bde	
	28/3		Above officers returned. 8 Prece per Battery fused. Inget gun drivel	
	29/3		C.O. Adjt. B.C's, Captains, 41 Subalterns attached to Batteries in firing line	
	31/3		C.O. Adjt. Captains returned. Lecture by Gen. Wyngham.	

J. R. Chumley
Lieut. Col. Comdg.
7th London Brigade, R.F.A.

121/5099

2nd London Division

7th London Brigade R.F.A.

Vol II 1 - 28.4.15

WAR DIARY
or
INTELLIGENCE SUMMARY.

(Erase heading not required.)

Army Form C. 2118.

7th London B'de R.F.A.

7th LONDON BRIGADE, R.F.A.
30 APR 1915

Place	Date	Hour	Summary of Events and Information	Remarks and references to Appendices
Auchel	1/4/15		C.O. Adjt & Captains returned to Michel. Lecture at CRA's H.Qrs. by Gen. Brigham.	
"	2/4/15		Major Read, Major Mead & 2 Lt. returned. Telephone laid to CRA.	
"	3/4/15		Aeroplane passed over at 12.30 am. Church Parade.	
"	4/4/15		Church Parade. 7.G.CM. Conference of O.Ps.C. at Brit H.Q.	
"	5/4/15		Divisional Canteens and Shoemakers & Tailors shops started at Allouagne. 660 Sand bags received.	
"	6/4/15		Brigade route march. Capt Callaghan attached to 34 Bde HQ.	
"	7/4/15		2 Telephonists per H.Q & L/Bdr & Bdr attached to 34 Bde. L/Bdr Roberts returned from St Venant.	
"			645. No 65 Fuzes received from 5th Dep. 7.A. 13th.	
"	8/4/15		Adjt Orderly Officer & NCO to Dep Supply & Tel Supps. S.Sgt Skillington lined by Bde.	
"	9/4/15		2 officers and 48 men per battery to 34 H.Bde to prepare positions.	
"	10/4/15		Capt Callaghan returned from attachment.	
Camblin	11/4/15		18th & 19th Btys & H.Q. moved into positions near 9.1k + 10.15 Agp. 20 Btys returned to Michel.	
"	12/4/15		19th Bty registering on F.177 - 13aing House & locations. 9 Fuges from Salas 200 2nd Cast.	
"			18th Bty registering on the Triangle in the afternoon. Allowance 12 rds per battery for day.	
	13/4/15		Bty. Commanders reconnoitering. 20th Bty inspection by Sir D. Haig.	
	14/4/15		Batteries continued registering. Col Renwick (14th + 15th) returned from leave and assumed Command of 7th L.Bde. Moved to Firfay. Col Lambert. All rds received to 75 rounds per gun for day.	

WAR DIARY or INTELLIGENCE SUMMARY

Army Form C. 2118.

Place	Date	Hour	Summary of Events and Information	Remarks and references to Appendices
CAMBRIN	15/4/15		18th Battery continued registering. 19th Bty did night firing (12 rounds). Capt. Marshall	
"	16/4/15		to G.H.Q. H.Qrs. Flying Corps for course.	
"	17/4/15		Batteries continued registering. 32 Remounts received at Chocques	
"	18/4/15		19th Bty vacated and 20th Bty took their place.	
"	19/4/15		20th Bty commenced registering.	
"	20/4/15		20th Bty continued registering.	
"	21st		Cpls Warn British & Nagy Tyler for course received.	
"	22nd		19th Bty instructed to report to 15th to 16th Div. 1st Plate on Rev Zouave	
"	23rd		19th Bty took over 4 Gun Emplacements of 16th R.F.A. & depobed.	
"	24th		19th Bty vacated position on S. side of Taming Fork, and ofs/1920	
"	25th		Lt. Agnew killed	
"	26th		28th Lt. Doak attached to CRA's Staff	
"	27th		1 Section 15th Bty moved to position S of Gorre Caves	
"	28th		26th Depn line shells 4 shrun shells & 1 round	
			Capt Marshall returned from G.H.Q.	

121/5573

44th Division.

7th London Bde. R.F.A.

Vol III 1 — 31.5.15

Army Form C. 2118.

WAR DIARY
or
INTELLIGENCE SUMMARY.
(Erase heading not required.)

4th London Bde (howitzer) RFA. May 1915

Instructions regarding War Diaries and Intelligence Summaries are contained in F. S. Regs., Part II. and the Staff Manual respectively. Title pages will be prepared in manuscript.

Place	Date	Hour	Summary of Events and Information	Remarks and references to Appendices
CAMBRIN	1st.		19th. Hows. Bty. moved to CORBIE — came into action at S bend in TUNING FORK W.A. MARAIS LE PLANTAIN — registered	7M13
	2nd.		All wires fuzes returned to D.A.C.	7x13
	3rd.		Leading wagons into state of ammunition. The brigade were stopped firing. F.G.C.M. Gunner Barr, 19th How. Batty.	f x13
	6th.		War Pongs at left over. Bde. came into group under command of Lt. Col. Graham R.J.A. Major Manyot gave up adjutancy & returned to 116th Batty R.F.A. Lieut. S.A. Buchan took over duties of Adjutant. Conference of C.O. of Div. Arty. Cols, Te, 2to.	f x13
	7th.		Registration fuzes in front of German trenches by 18th + 10th Batteries	
		5pm	19th. Bty. fired guns at request of infy to disturb bombing.	9Dx13
	8th.		Registration of wire entanglements in morning. 18th Bty. fired afternoon, at request of Infy to stop German shooting of KEEP.	fp13
	9th.	4.10 am	19th Bty. Slow gun fire on wire in front of trenches. Storm to & bailiff G., later attack must be running on our front, but insufficient ammunition returned — no reply	
		?	19th. Bty. took part in bombardment of FESTUBERT front	
		6.55 am	Objective changed to LABASSEE ROAD behind German trenches in front of our left of front of Reuters Barn.	7x13

1577 Wt.W10791/1773 500,000 1/15 D.D.&L. A.D.S.S./Forms/C. 2118.

WAR DIARY or INTELLIGENCE SUMMARY

Army Form C. 2118.

1st London Brigade R.F.A.   May 1915.

Place	Date	Hour	Summary of Events and Information	Remarks and references to Appendices
			Set/out then to economise ammunition. French attack S. of LA BASSEE ROAD towards LOOS [transparent were - own in RICHEBOURG front held up. 8 Remounts received.	See A.P.B
	10th.		Quiet day - occasional rounds during day on to comm. trenches & second line. German Batteries shelled CAMBRIN - adjacent to H.Q.	See A.P.B
	11th.	11.55am	18th. "20th Btys fired to support left of french attack. German replied by shelling CAMBRIN and ANNEQUIN	See A.P.B
		2.30pm	14th Bty. engaged a silenced German Bty. at A 22 b 33	
		9pm	Chappear fired 12 rounds into CAMBRIN.	
	12th.		2/Lt. C.B.Ruson reports for duty from Base Details - to Ammn. Column. Lee HADFIELD sheer at 63 Lys returned to D.A.C.	
	13th.	12.30pm	German Howitzer Battery shelled CUINCHY. In accordance with general instruction received from 1st Army re annoying the enemy both Batteries shelled roads and road junctions in rear of German lines.	See A.P.B See A.P.B
	14th.		Above practice continued	

WAR DIARY
or
INTELLIGENCE SUMMARY.

(Erase heading not required.)

Army Form C. 2118.

7th London Brigade R.F.A.

May 1915

Place	Date	Hour	Summary of Events and Information	Remarks and references to Appendices
	16th.		J.O.M. inspected guns. 1 gun of 18th. + 1 of 20th. condemned as unserviceable. Quiet day.	
		11pm	In accordance with instructions received for supporting night attack, 18th. + 20th. Btys. opened a slow rate of fire on Ger. trenches between LA BASSEE ROAD and "Brickstacks" withdrawal of gun fire at 11.30 p.m. and 11.35 p.m. Slow rate maintained until 3.15 a.m. when another burst. from 3.15 a.m. till daylight a slow rate again on road junction E.23 and on road about F.16. 19th. Bty. supported attack of 7th. Division on FESTUBERT front. The movement of enemy on our immediate front 98.M. continued. Fire of 19th. Bty. Occasional bursts from 18th. + 20th. Btys. during day on road junction E.23 4 am - noon East of AUCHY (E.23 - E.24)	to A.B [?] 7
	17th.		Quiet day on our front. Heavy firing and some progress N. of GIVENCHY. 19th. Bty. supported N. of CANAL	to A.B [?]
	17th/18th. 11.30p- 18th.	(18th)	In accordance with instructions from Head Quarters 18th. + 20th. Btys. fired short bursts of fire to make it appear in rear of German lines, until daylight. Both Btys. registered on roads (H.29 - J.24) in CANTELEUX to support attack N.E. of GIVENCHY when cancelled. Quiet day.	to A.B [?]
	19th.		Quiet day. German shelled PONT FIXE at about 2 p.m.	to A.B [?]

WAR DIARY or INTELLIGENCE SUMMARY

Army Form C. 2118.

1st London Brigade R.F.A.

May 1915

Place	Date	Hour	Summary of Events and Information	Remarks and references to Appendices
		5.40 p.m	18th. Bty. engaged and silenced battery at A22.B.3.3. firing down LA BASSEE road. Single gun of 15th. Bty. was entrenched by 18th. 6.P. to enfilade CANTELEUX communication trenches. 18th. Bty. went into rest at FONTENELLE FARM. (one gun to 20th. – two guns to 19th. † damaged gun returned to BAC) Col. Blanier took command of Artillery, A Section, 4/L. Divnl. Amn. (20th Res. Bty.)	L F B
	20th.	12.20 p.m	Single gun 18th. Row Bty, 50th. Bty. R.F.A. SL/J. (Low) Bty. R.F.A. In reponse to a message from 34th. Bde. that our trenches at GIVENCHY were being enfiladed from TRIANGLE, 20th. Battery engaged German battery located at A22 & B.3.3.	
		11 p.m	Heavy bombardment of our trenches N. of GIVENCHY – 20th. Battery fired on CANTELEUX communication trenches and roads. From 8 p.m to 10½ p.m. 20th. Battery shelled CANTELEUX roads in endeavour to stop supports coming up.	H F B
	31st.	5.15 am	In accordance with instructions 20th. Bty. fired 50 rds. at mine at E.3.	
		1.40 p.m	20th. Bty. fired a few rounds on to trenches (EO to stop bombing, at request of Infantry.)	
		4 p.m	20th. Bty. fired slowly on to mine (E3) to complete and widen gap. Single gun 18th. Bty. registered trenches S.9. S.8. H.10. H.4. H.13.	
		7.30 p.m	Bombardment in accordance with instructions – Single gun on trenches registered.	

WAR DIARY or INTELLIGENCE SUMMARY

Army Form C. 2118.

5. 7th Ronden Bougade R.F.A.

May 1915

Place	Date	Hour	Summary of Events and Information	Remarks and references to Appendices
	22nd		20th Bty. on CANTELEUX road (K.29. I.24)	L.A.B.
		6.30am	Heavy German bombardment of our trenches N. of GIVENCHY - 20th Bty. fired on CANTELEUX	
			Col. Carey R.F.A. took over command of Group from Col. Chambers.	L.A.B.
	23rd	12 noon	German 5.9" How. Shelling KEEP - 20th Bty. retaliated by shelling communication trench	
			between C. & D. billets Kalio. In afternoon single gun (9.4) continued registration.	L.A.B.
	24th		Quiet day. Single gun continued registration.	L.A.B.
	26th	3pm - 4.45pm	Single gun kept up steady rate of fire on CANTELEUX - VIOLAINES road.	
			Quiet on our front.	L.A.B.
	26th		Quiet day. 20th Bty. fired occasionally to check ranging.	L.A.B.
	27th		Quiet day. 19th Bty. moved into position at CUINCHY	L.A.B.
	28th		Quiet on our front, 19th Bty. registered on GIVENCHY front from new position	L.A.B.
	29th		20th Bty. moved to C.W.Flanders of TUNING FORK & came under Col. Home. Single gun withdrawn	
			Hd. Bde. moved to FONTENELLE FERME having no batteries.	L.A.B.
	30th		Quiet day	L.A.B.
	31st		O.C. & Adjt. went to reconnoitre positions for 19th & 20th near VERMELLES. One section	
			each of 19th & 20th withdrawn to wagon lines.	L.A.B.

F.A. Buchan
Lieut. R.F.A. Adjt.
for O.C. 7th London R.F.A.

47th Division.

18/6/15

7th London Bde R.F.A.

Vol IV 1-30.6.15.

a2
a96

Army Form C. 2118.

WAR DIARY
or
INTELLIGENCE SUMMARY.

7th London Brigade R.F.A.
June 1915

(Erase heading not required.)

Instructions regarding War Diaries and Intelligence Summaries are contained in F.S. Regs., Part II. and the Staff Manual respectively. Title pages will be prepared in manuscript.

Place	Date	Hour	Summary of Events and Information	Remarks and references to Appendices
NOELLES	June 1st		19/20th Batteries & Bde B.Kn. moved up into action in vicinity of NOEULLES-LES-VERMELLES. Wagon Lines at Chateau NOEULLES-LES-VERMELLES. Bde. Am. Col. at VERQUIGNEUL.	S.A.B.
	2nd		19th/20th Btys. registered on German trenches	S.A.B.
			16th Battery (in reserve) brought up to chateau of NOEULLES. 19th Battery fired on German working party	S.A.B.
	3rd 4th		Registration continued.	S.A.B.
			18th Battery moved back to DROUVIN. Left Section 19th Bty moved to rear position at GRENAY in relief of 17th Bty 3 R.F.A., taking over new ammunition in route. Quiet day	S.A.B.
	5th		R. Section 19th Bty battery moved to join L.X. at GRENAY. Registration commenced by L x 2 - 19th Battery	S.A.B.
	6th		18th Battery moved from DROUVIN to KIERRETTES 19th Battery continued registration. All quiet on 20th Bty Z	S.A.B.
	7th			S.A.B.

1577 W† W/6795/1773 500,000 1/15 D.D.&L. A.D.S.S./Forms/C. 2118.

Army Form C. 2118.

WAR DIARY
or
INTELLIGENCE SUMMARY.
(Erase heading not required.)

Place	Date	Hour	Summary of Events and Information	Remarks and references to Appendices
AMES	8th		Quiet day.	
		4pm	H.Q. 20th F.B.2 & Bde A.C. Geo S.A.A section went into rest at AMES. S.A.A section moved to ROUVIN.	App B
	9th		Rest.	App B
	10th		Rest. Capts F.J. Callaghan transferred to home establishment. Lieut R.T. Clegg posted to command A.C. from 20th F.B.2.	App B
	11th		Rest.	App B
	12th		Rest.	App B
	13th–14th		19th F.B.2 carried out further registration of fixed at request of infantry to stop bombing. 19th F.B.2 took part in a bombardment of German 1st & 2nd line trenches & communication trenches.	App B
	15th		Remainder of F.B.2 in rest at AMES. 1st H.F. Scranton posted from A.C. to 20th F.B.2. 19th Battery had one gun put out of action & one horse damaged by H.E. Shell.	App B
	16th		Quiet day.	App B

WAR DIARY or INTELLIGENCE SUMMARY

Army Form C. 2118.

Place	Date	Hour	Summary of Events and Information	Remarks and references to Appendices
	17th		18th B Battery personnel relieved 19th B[attery] in action at TRENAY. (L.36.a.4.5)	App B
	18th		19th B[attery] moved into rest at PIERRETTES.	App B
	19th		Quiet day.	App B
	20th		Quiet day. 1st Lt. Guthrie R.A.M.C. injured.	App B
	21st		Quiet day	App B
	22nd		22nd Capt. Whitehead RAMC took over medical charge.	App B
	23rd		Quiet day	App B
LAPUGNOY	24th		H.Q. 19th B., 20th B. & half O.C. injured crews billets at LAPUGNOY.	App B
	25th		Rest	
	26th		26th Corpl. G. Harris and Bomb. H. Richards 19th Battery awarded D.C.M. 18th Battery replied to heavy shelling of own trenches by firing on German trenches. 10.30 p.m. 18th B. fired to disperse German working party.	App B
	27th		All quiet.	
	28th			
	29th			
	30th			

D1/6427

47th Division

1/7th London Bde R.F.A.

Vol I

From 1st to 31st July 1915

7th London Brigade R.F.A.

Instructions regarding War Diaries and Intelligence Summaries are contained in F. S. Regs., Part II. and the Staff Manual respectively. Title pages will be prepared in manuscript.

WAR DIARY
or
INTELLIGENCE SUMMARY.
(Erase heading not required.)

Army Form C. 2118.

Place	Date	Hour	Summary of Events and Information	Remarks and references to Appendices
POUGNY	July 1st		⎫ Brigade in Rest at POUGNOY. 18th Battery in action at GRENAY	7/A/B
	2nd		⎪	7/A/B
	3rd		⎬ H.A. Capt P.G. Cooper 18th Bty wounded	7/A/B
	4th		⎪	
	5th 6th		⎭ Brigade in Rest. 18th B'ty - in action	7/A/B
	7th		O.C. 20th Battery reconnoitred position near GRENAY. Single gun of 20th Battery into action in evening for registration next day.	7/A/B
	8th		7.A.M. Bdon joined from Base & posted to Ammn Column. 20th Battery single gun registered.	7/A/B
GRENAY	9th		Bde HQ & remainder of 20th moved up into action at GRENAY in relief of French Artillery. Col Chambers took over at 11 pm Command of the Group covering N section. HQ at Chateau at GRENAY. 19th Bty remained in rest at POUGNOY	7/A/B
	10th		Registration continued by 20th B'ty	7/A/B
	11th		Bde A.C. camped at DROUVIN. Retaliation at various times for shelling of billets. 10th B	7/A/B
	12th		Orders received in morning for relief of Bde by S Midland R.F.A Cancelled at 9 p.m. Retaliation	7/A/B

Army Form C. 2118.

WAR DIARY
or
INTELLIGENCE SUMMARY.
(Erase heading not required.)

Instructions regarding War Diaries and Intelligence Summaries are contained in F. S. Regs., Part II and the Staff Manual respectively. Title pages will be prepared in manuscript.

Place	Date	Hour	Summary of Events and Information	Remarks and references to Appendices
GRENAY	13th	11am - 5pm	Intermittent shelling by Germans of area S.W. of Grenay with heavy shells, apparently looking for French batteries in action there.	App B
	14th	6.15pm - 7.30pm	Heavy bombardment by French on our immediate front of German lines. Retaliation during day. Capt W. Kitchener R.A.M.C. returned to 5th London F.A. being relieved as M.O. of brigade by Lt. M. McKeown R.A.M.C.	App B
	15th		} Quiet days. Certain amount of retaliation of German billets & trenches for shelling & bombing of ours	—
	16th			App B
	17th			—
	18th			App B
	19th		Quiet day. Working party (40 men) from 19th B² came up to work on gun positions under 6th London Brigade R.F.A.	App B
	20th		Enemy shelled Fosse 6 (about 500x from the town & in rear of 18th B²) with 10 inch gun. No steps taken, by Germans. (9.15am - 2pm).	App B
	21st		Quiet day. Retaliation.	
	22nd		3/1st R.G. Coates joined from Base. Transfer to Army (L⁴ Lt. J. Simmonds transferred from Remount to 18th B².	App B

1577 Wt.W10791/1773 500,000 1/15 D.D.&L. A.D.S.S./Forms/C. 2118.

Army Form C. 2118.

WAR DIARY
or
INTELLIGENCE SUMMARY.
(Erase heading not required.)

Place	Date	Hour	Summary of Events and Information	Remarks and references to Appendices
GRENAY	23rd		Quiet day. Retaliation.	to A3
	24th			to A3
	25th		25th normal hostile aeroplane activity about 6.15 pm	to A3
	26th		Quiet day. Retaliation.	to A3
	27th		27th Capt E.H. Blood, 75 Bde (Roy) attached to 20th Battery	
	28th		Quiet day. One section 18th B13 relieved by 'A' Battery 72 W.Bry ada Kim at 11.30 pm	to A3
			Quiet day. Remaining section 18th B13 relieved at 11pm. 4½ section 25th at 11.15 pm by "B" battery.	to A3
	29th		Quiet day. Bde HQ relieved by HQ 72nd Bde RFA. Relief 07.30 Battery completed. Capt Stocking took over from Col Chambers at 12 noon. 19th Battery joined Bde at 9.05 Hrs.	to A3
GoSWAY	30th 31st		Bde in rest at 9.05 NAY.	to A3

FAT Brohan
Capt RFA
Adjt 17th Bde RFA (Howitzer)

47th Division

1/5th London Bde R.F.A.
Vol VI
August 15.

1/6781

WAR DIARY
or
INTELLIGENCE SUMMARY

7th London Brigade R.F.A.

Army Form C. [stamp: 9 SEP 1915]

Place	Date	Hour	Summary of Events and Information	Remarks and references to Appendices
GOSNAY	August 1st to 8th		Batteries & Bde HQ in rest. In accordance with instructions from Gen² 2nd Army Bde was made in training A.C orders on Battery work	ApB
	9th		Brigade Sports on racecourse at HESDIGNEUL. General Sir Douglas Haig & Genl. Rawlinson attended.	ApB
	15th		Working party of 2 Officers & 100 men sent up to 7th FA Bde B.S.	ApB
102 ING HEM CHATEAU	12th 15th		Brigade moved to ROZINGHEM CHATEAU. Remain in rest there	ApB
	16th		Major C. Head from 18th Lon Bde RFA to command 47th Div A.C. Capt H.G. Marshall from 19th Lon B³ RFA to command 18th Lon B³ RFA. 1st R.B. Allman from England posted to 20th Lon B³ RFA. 1st Lt H.C. Drewitton from 20th Lon B³ RFA attached to Bde HQ for instrus in duties of Adjutant	ApB
	16th - 19th		Bde in rest. 19th 2nd Lt H.C.B. Kinder attached from 47th Div Amm Col posted to 19th Bde Capt G.F. Bartholomew S.C. & Joined Bde. Two 18pr. guns from A Battery 72nd Bde sent for use purposes	ApB
	21st		2nd Lt O. Edwardes from England posted to A.C.	ApB

WAR DIARY
or
INTELLIGENCE SUMMARY.
(Erase heading not required.)

Army Form C. 2118

Place	Date	Hour	Summary of Events and Information	Remarks and references to Appendices
OZIEVIERY	23rd		Capt H.E. Wood from 47" R.F.A. posted to 19th How. B? R.F.A.	to A.B
	24th		Inspection of Transport by O.C. 47 & D Train	to A.B
	25th		47th Fiv.l Sports at ALLOUAGNE.	to A.B
	26th		Conference of C.Os & Adjutants at OHATEAU LOZINGHEM at 9am.	to A.B
			Lt R.G. Burges from 20th How B? R.F.A. to 19th How B? R.F.A	
			Lt S.E. Raley from 19th How. to 20th How B? R.F.A	
	31st		Lt L.C.G. Burgess attached for duty to 25" Bde R.F.A at	to A.B
			NOYELLES.	

for Buckam
    Capt R.F.A.
Adjt 7th How Brigade R.F.A

Weekly Strength Return — 4th London Brigade R.F.A.

Sunday - 6th June 1915

UNITS	A FIGHTING STRENGTH		B Detaches on Col. and other details with unit		C Excused duty under Col. orders		D Kit Strength		E Horses/mules		F Remarks
	OFF	O.R.	OFF	O.R.	OFF	O.R.	Present	Horses	Riding	Other	
Bde. H.Q.	3	25	1	4	-	-	34	2	34		
10th Co. Ldn. Bde.	4	149	-	5	-	-	141	-	125	+1 on course at C.C.S.
19th Co. Ldn. Bde.	4	138	-	15	-	-	126	-	122	+1 major seconded to G.R.F.C.
20th Co. Ldn. Bde.	4	119	-	8	-	-	131	-	126	
4th Co. Ldn. A/C	4	141	1	4	-	-	141	96	33	+1 on course C.C.T.S.
Total	19	527	1	36	-	-	577	98	439	

Weekly Strength Return of 7th Howitzer Brigade R.F.A.

Friday 13th August 1915

20/8/15

UN 115	A. Fighting Strength		B. Individual Col. Att. not actually with unit		C. Draft received since last return		D. Ration Strength			E. Explanation of any discrepancy between fighting strength known other than on this return and that on last
	OFF.	O.R.	OFF.	O.R.	OFF.	O.R.	Personnel	Horses & mules heavy	Other horses & mules	
Bde. H.Qrs.	3	34*	—	6	—	—	35	2	34	*1 man wounded
15th How. Batty.	4	140	1	32	—	—	141	—	125	
19th How. Batty.	4	134*	—	40	—	1	138	1	132	*3 men have joined from 7th Lon. A.C. 1 man wounded
20th How. Batty.	4	139	—	33	—	—	134	—	126	
7th Lon. A.C.	4	135*	—	35	—	3	64?	94	33	*3 Reinforcement from Base 3 men have joined 19th Lon. Bty.
Total	19	588	1	146	—	3	580	96	440	

Col. B. includes working park of 1 Officer + 146 other Ranks

Captain R.F.A.
Adjt 7th (London) Brigade R.F.A.

Weekly Strength Return of 7th London Brigade R.F.A.

Thursday 19th August 1915

UNIT	A. Fighting Strength	B. Included in Col A but detached with Div.		C. Staff records base details retained		D. Ration Strength		E. Explanation for divergency between fighting strength shown in this return and that on last.
	O.R.	OFF.	O.R.	OFF.	O.R.	Personnel	Horses mules & Donkeys	Other horses and mules	
Bde. H.Qrs.	3	–	–	–	–	38	2	33	
18th Lon Batty	4	140	–	4	–	134	–	126	+2 men transferred from 19th Lon Batty
19th Lon Batty	4	132	–	7	32½	126	–	122	{+2 men transferred to Base Details, 18th Lon Btty, 4/1st Lon Div Ammn 4/1st D.A.C. ; 1 man from 18th Btty, 1 man from 20th Btty
20th Lon Batty	4	137	–	3	1	132	–	123	½
7th Lon A.C.	4	133	–	2	2	134	99	33	+5 N.C.O. men evacuated 8 out of Divl Area
Total	19	676	–	21	12½	564	101	437	

Col. B. includes working parties of 2 Officers and 82 other ranks

P.T.O.

Captain R.F.A.
Adjt 7th (London) Brigade, R.F.A.

Weekly Strength Return of 7th London Brigade R.F.A.
Thursday 26th August 1915

UNITS	A. Fighting Strength		B. Included in Col A, but not actually with unit		C. Drafts received since last return		D. Ration Strength			E. Explanation of any discrepancy between Fighting Strength shown in this return and that on last.
	OFF.	O.R.	OFF.	O.R.	OFF.	O.R.	Personnel	Heavy Draught Horses	Other horses and mules	
Bde. H.Q.	4*	36°	-	3	-	-	41	2	33	*Capt H.E. Wood transferred from 4/A Div. a/c 23/8/15 - not yet posted to D.A.C. ° 2 men transferred to D.A.C.
18th Lon. Batt.	4	136+	-	26	-	-	137	-	126	+3 O.R. recruits from Lond. C. D.A.C.
19th Lon. Batt.	4	127+	4	26	-	-	129	-	118	+6 O.R. recruits 1 O.R. transferred from D.A.C.
20th Lon. Batt.	4	133+	-	28	-	-	131	-	122	+3 O.R. recruited 1 O.R. discharged
7th Lon. A.C.	5*	134+	1	22	1	-	133	99	34	*2/Lieut G.B. Edwards joined from England 21/8/15 +2 returned from hospital, 1 after absence of evacuation had been received.
Total	21	666	3	104	1	-	571	101	433	

Col. B. includes Ashrey Park of 26 Officers & 82 Other ranks

Captain R.F.A.
Adj. 7th (London) Brigade R.F.A.

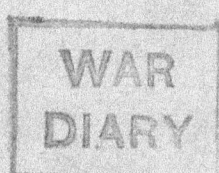

Headquarters,

237th BRIGADE, R.F.A.
(1/7 London)

(47th Division)

S E P T E M B E R

1 9 1 5

Attached:

Weekly Strength Returns.

War Diary (September 1915)
7 A(Ln) Brigade R.F.A.

Army Form C. 2118

WAR DIARY
or
INTELLIGENCE SUMMARY

(Erase heading not required.)

Place	Date	Hour	Summary of Events and Information	Remarks and references to Appendices
LOZINGHEM	Sept 1st		Brigade moved to bivouacs in fields S.W. of Bois des Dames. Bac-mood	App 13
BOIS DES DAMES	2nd		to TAILLECOURT.	
	3rd		Major Gerald & Lt. Raley to France for duty as Observing Officers with McNAUGHTAN Group. All went out to R.A. Survey Northern front working with McNAUGHTAN Group.	App 13 App 13
	4th		18 pr gun cart for instructions returned to 15 pr 2 att.	
	5th		4th L.A. Bingas attached 39 B. Batt for ration	
	6th		6th Capt. (Hy) Transferred to England (sick)	
	7th		Lt. Edwardes to command R.A. Survey MAG 2 in 7 MR B.E.	
	8th		Brigade attend	
	9th			
	10th			
	11th			
	12th			App 13
	13th			
	14th			
	15th			

WAR DIARY
or
INTELLIGENCE SUMMARY.

Army Form C. 2118

Place	Date	Hour	Summary of Events and Information	Remarks and references to Appendices
POIS DES DAMES	16th		Brigade at rest.	to A13
	17th		16th A Battery moved into action at Gernery in relief of G B13 RHA	to A13
	18th		R! Section 19th joined 15th in action forming six gun battery under Capt Marshall. 19th & 16th R.S. Registration. Maj'r R A Coates attached 25th Bde 13n for duty.	to A13
	19th		18th B13 continued Registration.	to A13
			1 Section of 20th B13 moved into action (detached) in 111946C.	to A13
	20th		Major Peal attached to Liason officer with 14th R.L. Int. Bn.	
	21st		First day of Bombardment [IV] 15th B13 took part. 20th Section (System) Bde H.Q. to registr. 14th Sections 17, 19 & 26 B13's moved up to	R A i.
HAILLICOURT	22nd		HAILLICOURT [C] Chemin - O.C. Reserve Artillery. 1st Pitzdyd attacked with 6th hon Rgt. ao 400.	to A13
			Second day of Bombardment [IV]. 16 & B13 took part. Mt. T. Iron & Lieut N.C.O's men detached to duty with Armoured Car Section.	
	23rd		Third day of Bombardment [X]. 18th B13 took part. Orders for Bde in case of Advance	to A13

WAR DIARY or INTELLIGENCE SUMMARY

Army Form C. 2118

Place	Date	Hour	Summary of Events and Information	Remarks and references to Appendices
Hulluch	24th		Fourth day of Bombardment [M] 15th BA took front part [Z] Attack launched 18th BA fired on our trenches 5.30 am to 8.15 am continuously. Enemy heavy day. 20th BA Lostin fired on our trenches. Reserve Artillery moved up to 75s B20 B15	to App 13
	25th		18th BA fired on our front line trenches during day & on our trenches at night. Enemy reports of hostile barrage for counterattacks. 20th BA ditto.	to App 13
	26th		15th BA as yesterday. 20th BA A wounded in tommy Southern barrage. Captain Buchan died & Lons to Lonte Rendez Vous	to App 13
	27th		Guns in front & seen located. 15th BA fired occasionally during day. Ten machineguns not of right. 20th BA ditto - Barrage gun. Capt. Buchan again to Tons S. fire guns from M.G.s Trenery. Two Count & manned by 15th BA.	to App 13
	28th		15th BA quiet day - Considerable sightening on front line, House lines in Les BREBIS Château - no casualties.	to App 13
	30th		18th BA quiet day - one fixed gun to register	to App 13

J.R. Buchan
Capt. R.F.A.

1577 Wt. W10791/1773 500,000 1/15 D.D. & L. A.D.S.S./Forms/C. 2118.

WEEKLY STRENGTH RETURNS.

Weekly Strength Return of 7th London Brigade RFA

Thursday - 2nd September 1915

Unit	A. Fighting Strength		B. Ordered to Col. A but not actually with unit		C. Drafts received since last return		D. Rating Strength			E. Explanation of any discrepancy between fighting strength shown on this return and that on last
	OFF.	O.R.	OFF.	O.R.	OFF.	O.R.	Personnel	Horses & mules Heavy	Other horses and mules	
Bde. H.Qrs.	3*	34*	-	3	-	-	*3 +1	1	36	* Capt. W and 2 men shown on last return as unposted to 19th Lon. Batty.
19th Lon. Batty	4	135*	1	41	-	-	134	-	127	* 1 man discharged. Reminder 6 engagement
19th Lon. Batty	4	127*	2	52	-	-	128	-	118	2 men from H.Q. transferred to 19.85. 2 men evacuated (if strength) = Bdr. W and transferred from H.6. Rank Smoaton transferred to 20.85
20th Lon. Batty	5	128*	-	42	-	-	123	-	124	* 6 men wounded since last return. Rk. Smoaton transferred from 14/8/15
7th Lon. A.C.	5	133*	2	37	-	-	134	99	34	* 1 man to Base for recharge
Total	21	557	6	175	-	-	560	100	+39	

Col. B. includes working party 141
Teleffrum & Lon Coll. Center

Weekly Strength Return 7th. London Brigade R.F.A.

Thursday, 9th September, 1915

Unit	A. Fighting Strength		B. Included in Col. A, but actually since last return with unit		C. Drafts received since last return		D. Ration Strength				E. Explanation of any discrepancy between fighting strength shown in this return and that on last
	OFF.	O.R.	OFF.	O.R.	OFF.	O.R.	Personnel	Horses Heavy	Horses & mule Draft	Other horses & mules	
6te. L.Bde.	3	33*	-	7	-	-	41	1		36	* 1 man transferred to Brit. Battalion staff
15th. Lon. Bte.	4	133*	-	10	-	-	129	-		124	* 2 men evacuated
19th. Lon. Bte.	4	126*	3	14	-	-	123	-		116	* 1 man evacuated
208. Lon. Bte.	5	128	2	30	-	-	132	-		126	
7th. Lon. A.C.	5	133	2	36	-	-	112	74		33	
Total	21	563	7	96	-	-	537	75		434	

Captain R.F.A.
Adjt 7th (London) Brigade R.F.A.

Weekly Strength Return

7th. London Brigade R.F.A.

Thursday, 16th. September. 1915

UNIT.	A. Fighting Strength		B. Included in A. but not actually with unit		C. Drafts received since last return		D. Ration Strength			E. Explanation of any difference between fighting strength shown and that on last
	OFF.	O.R.	OFF.	O.R.	OFF.	O.R.	Personnel	Horses Heavy	Horses Draught & Riding	
Bde. H.Qrs.	3	32*	-	1	-	-	37	1	33	*1 man sent to Base for discharge
Rd. Am. Batty	4	133	-	8	-	-	131	-	124	
19th. Am. Batty	4	127†	3	29	-	-	116	-	116	†2 men rejoined from Base 1 man recruited to Base
20th. Am. Batty	5	135‡	2	30	-	6	126	-	124	‡ Draft received from Base 6 1 man rejoined from Base Hospital 1
7th. Am. A.C.	5	141‡	2	40	-	6	118	74	32	‡ Draft received from Base 6 Recruits from Base rejoined 2/8
Total	21	568	7	114	-	12	527	75	429	

A.M. Buchan
Captain R.F.A.
Adjt 7th (London) Brigade R.F.A.

7th London Brigade R.F.A.

Weekly Strength Return

Thursday 23rd September 1915

23 SEP 1915

Unit	A. Fighting Strength		B. Detached in one capacity or another but with unit at its ultimate destination		C. Staff regimental & extra regimental		Ration Strength			E. Estimated flying deadweight including fats themselves and detail in rear
	OFF	O.R.	OFF	O.R.	OFF	O.R.	Personnel	Horses Heavy	Riding Draught and under	
Bde. H.Q.	3	32	-	8	-	-	34	1	34	
15th Co. Ron. Bty.	4	132*	-	8	-	-	134	-	122	*
16th Co. Ron. Bty.	4	128*	3	18	-	-	142	-	122	*
17th Co. Ron. Bty.	5	134*	3	9	-	-	128	-	122	*
4th Ron. A.C.	4*	140	3	42	-	-	110	68	29	*
Total	20	566	9	85	-	-	515	69	428	

Captain R. F. A.
Adjt. 7th (London) Brigade R.F.A.

Weekly Strength Return of 1st Canadian Brigade R.F.A.

Thursday 30th September 1915

Unit	A. Fighting Strength		B. Details at Brigade A. Train etc with rest		C. Details in hospital etc		D. Ration Strength			E. Remarks
	OFF	OR	OFF	OR	OFF	OR	Personnel	Horses & Mules Heavy	Horses & Mules Draught	
Bde H.Q.	3	32	-	8	-	-	34	1	34	
11th Can RG	4	130	-	1	-	-	129	-	123	
19th Can By	4	117	3	17	-	-	107	-	120	
20th Can By	5	137	4	10	-	-	106	-	119	
1st Can Am Col	4	140	2	31	-	-	111	67	30	
Total	20	566	9	73	-	-	487	68	426	

121/7439

47th Division

7th London Bde R.F.A.
Vol VIII
Oct 15

WAR DIARY or INTELLIGENCE SUMMARY

Army Form C. 2118.

7th Ldn Brigade R.F.A.

October 1915

Place	Date	Hour	Summary of Events and Information	Remarks and references to Appendices
LES BREBIS	1st		18 A Bty & 1 section 19 Bty relieved by French at 6 a.m., rejoined Bde at LES BREBIS. Bde (less section 20B, in action) marched to	
			1st DESIGNEUX. Bivouaced on Racecourse. Section of 20th rejoined in evening. Six hours notice to move.	to MB
AES DIGNEUX	2nd		Quiet day.	to MB
	3rd		7th Divn. and 8 men rejoined from Armoured Car Section	to MB
			Brigade marched to LABOURIERE	
LABOURIERE	4th		Quiet day	to MB
	5th		Orders to be ready to move at ½ hours notice. Telephones attached	to MB
			MAZINGARBEN GROUP regained.	
	6th		Orders to march to THELUS COURT, 11 a.m., changed en route & Bde	to MB
			moved to billets at MAZINGARBEN - LES - MINES	
MAZINGARBEN	7th		Quiet days — 8 2½ hours notice again for night.	to MB
	8th			
	9th		Inspection by Genl Rawlinson of representatives of units to proceed	
			at ROUILLY. 30 men per Bty — Colonel + Adjutant. Orders re further	to MB
			operations.	

WAR DIARY
or
INTELLIGENCE SUMMARY.

Army Form C. 2118.

Place	Date	Hour	Summary of Events and Information	Remarks and references to Appendices
MARIES	10th		Quiet day	App 13
	11th		G.O.C. 1st Army inspected horses for reclassification.	App 13
	12th		From 6 pm orders to move at short notice.	App 13
	13th		Quiet day.	App 13
	14th		Colonel & Adjt to MAZINGARBE to reconnoitre positions. Majors & digging parties to follow & spend night at PITKOSO PIRE. Starting work next day. Positions near LA RUTOIRE. Col Chambers Group. 14.15.19.20	App 13
	15th		Work started on positions. One section of 7.18.19.20 into action in the evening. Group to work under 15th Divl Artil — Lines of 7.15 pm on one trenches only.	App 13
PITKOSO PIRE	16th		Bde HQ move up to PITKOSO PIRE. Remainder of batteries into action. First sections in registered.	App 13
	17th		} Registration.	App 13
	18th			App 13
	19th		Registration of front line trenches — section of front to be taken over by Group (from) on 20th. Concentration of this on German front line at 3.0 pm.	App 13

Army Form C. 2118.

WAR DIARY
or
INTELLIGENCE SUMMARY.
(Erase heading not required.)

Instructions regarding War Diaries and Intelligence Summaries are contained in F. S. Regs., Part II. and the Staff Manual respectively. Title pages will be prepared in manuscript.

Place	Date	Hour	Summary of Events and Information	Remarks and references to Appendices
PHILOSOPHE	20th		Took over Section of front from 7am. 18pdrs going out of Scott positions — batteries to move to open positions. (not 14th)	to App 13
	21st		Registration. 15th move.	to App 13
	22nd		Chambers Group become Sub-Group under Colonel Scott. 15th, 14th & 20th on front line, with one 15pdr bty of 25th Bde on each sector. 14th Bty on line trenches. Scott Group under 47th Dvn.	to App 13
	23rd		Bombardment under Group orders at 11am & 11.30am. Registration proceeded with. 19th & 20th move.	to App 13
	24th		Registration. Bombardment 4.30 pm.	to App 13
	25th		"	to App 13
	26th		"	to App 13
	27th		Concentration of fire on German 2nd & 1st line 11am. 11.40am & 11.25am.	to App 13
	28th			
	29th		Bombardment under D.A. Corps arrangement 3am & 5am. Inspection by H.M. King George V at HAISNICOURT 10.30 am. Captn N.E. Wood to 30 men from Brigade.	to App 13
	30th		Quiet day.	to App 13
	31st			to App 13

for P Buckley
Capt RFA

47th Division

1/1 London Bde R.F.A.

1/1/
7636

Army Form C. 2118.

7th London Brigade R.F.A.(T)

WAR DIARY
or
INTELLIGENCE SUMMARY.
(Erase heading not required.)

November 1915

Instructions regarding War Diaries and Intelligence Summaries are contained in F. S. Regs., Part II. and the Staff Manual respectively. Title pages will be prepared in manuscript.

7TH LONDON BRIGADE, R.F.A.
30 NOV 1915

Place	Date	Hour	Summary of Events and Information	Remarks and references to Appendices
VERMELLES	1st		In action (Chambres sub group 14, 15, 19, 20 Btys.) - Scott Group VERMELLES	
	2nd		Shells during the morning. Scott Group bombardment	
	3rd		Scott Group bombardment	
	4th		Scott Group bombardment	
	5th		Scott Group bombardment	
			Lieut D.C. Mcneight attached to Royal Flying Corps. Capt S.A. Buchan transferred to 17th Division. B.D.R. 1st Army inspected H.D. Horses. One Salvo after every 2hrs day & night. 14th Battery moved out at night to CELLS in NOEUX-LES-MINES. Instructions for relaxation from IV Corps	
	6th		14th Battery exchanged 15 pdrs for 18 pdrs. 10. N.C.O + men of 7th HQ inspected by Lord Mayor of London at NAZINGARBE 12.30 pm. Bombardment round as on 5th Capt N.E. Wood. O.C. B&C wagon lines	
	7th		Lieut H.E.D. Kenton transferred from 47th Divisional Ammunition Column	
	8th		Scott Group bombardment	
	9th			
	10th			

Army Form C. 2118.

WAR DIARY
or
INTELLIGENCE SUMMARY.
(Erase heading not required.)

Instructions regarding War Diaries and Intelligence Summaries are contained in F.S. Regs., Part II and the Staff Manual respectively. Title pages will be prepared in manuscript.

Place	Date	Hour	Summary of Events and Information	Remarks and references to Appendices
VERMELLES	11th		Instructions for relief of the 47th Division by 1st Division received. Lieut H.S. Swanston appointed adjutant. Scott Group bombardment.	
	12th		Scott Group bombardment.	
	13th		Received instructions for relief of 47th Divisional Artillery. Scott Group bombardment.	
	14th		Received at NOEUX-LES-MINES Station 18 pr equipment + 12 gun limber wagons for B.A.C. Scott Group bombardment. One section of 18th, 19th + 25th Btys came out of action & billeted through at NOEUX-LES-MINES.	
	15th		Scott Group bombardment.	
	16th		Bde H.Q. moved in the afternoon to rest billets at CAUCHY-LA-TOUR. 2nd Section of 18th, 19th + 25th Btys moved out of action to NOEUX-LES-MINES. 1st Section of 18th, 19th + 25th Btys moved with their 18 pr equipment to rest billets. Handed over Bde H.Q. to Bgdr. Pass R.F.A. - 2nd/2nd T.G. g. Murphy + A.S. Wilkinson	
CAUCHY-LA-TOUR	17th		2nd Section of 18th, 19th + 25th Btys moved with new 18pr equipment from NOEUX-LES-MINES to rest billets at CAUCHY-LA-TOUR. B.A.C. also moved to rest billets. All 15pr gun + equipment were left at NOEUX-LES-MINES Station together with 6 G.S. wagons of the 73 A.C.	

WAR DIARY
or
INTELLIGENCE SUMMARY

Army Form C. 2118.

Place	Date	Hour	Summary of Events and Information	Remarks and references to Appendices
CAUCHY-LA-TOUR	17th		2nd Lieut P.H. Hodgson attached to 47th Divisional Signals.	
	18th		Rest. Fitted up 16pdr equipment.	
	19th		Lieut P.H. Pilditch attached to command B.A.C. Bde in rest	
	20		Bde in rest. Cairns in 16pdr, telephones, cooking, sanitation etc.	
	21			
	22			
	24			
	25		C.O - Col C.E. Clanton v.D left for England/Lt Col R. Peel in command.	
	26		Major Lord Savile in command of Bde during temporary absence of Major H.P. Peel.	
	27		Inspection of non-technical weapons by O.C. 47th Div train. L.D. horses for B.A.C. arrive.	
	28		Rest.	
	29		Orders for Divisional Rest travel received. Orders postponed 24 hours.	
	30		Further orders for Divisional Rest move but not received.	

H.E. Iwanitz
Lieut. R. Tattam
for O.C. 1st Home Bde. R.F.A.

7th London Bde R.F.A.

Dec /X/
vol

47

WAR DIARY or INTELLIGENCE SUMMARY

Army Form C. 2118.

Place	Date	Hour	Summary of Events and Information	Remarks and references to Appendices
RINCQ	1st		Divisional Route march. Left CAUCHY a la TOUR at 5.45 am. Joined in with advance guard infantry (under Col Fawkes) at St HILAIRE arrived RINCQ 4.30 pm	
CAUCHY a la TOUR	2nd		Divisional Route march. Returned to rest billets. Left RINCQ at 7.00 am and arrived CAUCHY a la TOUR at 2.30 pm	
"	3rd		Rest. Cleaning up after Divisional Route march	
"	4th		School of gunnery for Junior Officers & Senior N.C.Os recommenced at D.A.C. Auchel. 2 guns from the 19th Bty and 2 guns from 19th Bty with 4 Directors lent to D.A.C. for school of gunnery.	
"	5th		Rest. Fatigues on new horse standings etc. Capt Lloyd took Pixley to VSR.	
"	6th		-MELLES to see position to be occupied by 2nd Lon Bty. 2nd Lon Bty less guns (guns taken over from 5th Bty in position moved) up to Wagon line at NOEUX LES MINES and in the evening detachments went up to position just NORTH of VERMELLES. 2nd Bty guns taken over by 6th London J.A.B.	
"	7		Inspection at 1 oclock of 19th Lon Bty in full war marching order by C.R.A at AUCHEL. Inspection of remnants of the B.A.C by A.D.V.S	

Army Form C. 2118.

WAR DIARY
or
INTELLIGENCE SUMMARY.
(Erase heading not required.)

Instructions regarding War Diaries and Intelligence Summaries are contained in F.S. Regs., Part II. and the Staff Manual respectively. Title pages will be prepared in manuscript.

Place	Date	Hour	Summary of Events and Information	Remarks and references to Appendices
CAUCHY A LA TOUR	8th		1. Sub section (gun ammunition) under 2nd Lieut R.H. Coates went up to NOEUX LES MINES to relieve section of the 6th London B.A.C. & to supply 2nd Lon Bde with ammunition attached to 1st Division under 7th Bde R.H.A.	
"	9th		Brigade Route march in marching order.	
"	10th		All horses of the Brigade inspected by A.D.V.S.	
"	11th		Rest. General fatigues & exercise in gunnery etc.	
"	12th		Signal Comn. at 4th Corps and 47th Division closed. Information received that Field R. Moncrieff was posted to the R.F.C. on 9.12.15.	
"	13th		School of gunnery at D.A.C. finished. B.C.s went up by motor car to reconnoitre positions which they were taking over from 15 Division.	
"	14th		Conference of C.O. at C.R.A. 2nd Lieut L.B. Tansley joined from England. Lieut Hodgson & Elephinoats to new Bde H.Q. at SAILLY LA BOURSE.	
"	15th		Tansley posted to the Column & attached to 1st Lon Bty. Right section (guns only) under B.C. went up into positions. 19th Lon Bty at ANNEQUIN and 1st Lon Bty at VERMELLES.	
SAILLY LA BOURSE	16th		Bde H.Q. and remainder of 1st Lon Bty, 19th Lon Bty & B.A.C. went up into action.	

Army Form C. 2118.

WAR DIARY
or
INTELLIGENCE SUMMARY.

(*Erase heading not required.*)

Instructions regarding War Diaries and Intelligence Summaries are contained in F. S. Regs., Part II. and the Staff Manual respectively. Title pages will be prepared in manuscript.

Place	Date	Hour	Summary of Events and Information	Remarks and references to Appendices
SAILLY	17th		Inspection of lines by D.G.R.	
LABOURSE	18th		B.A.C. move from VERQUIN to NOEUX LES MINES joining up with the other Subsections.	
	19th		C.O. visits all gun positions.	
	20th		18th Bty in the Heavy Group, 19th Bty in the Lahore Group, 20th Bty in the Poole Group, continue battery work. Batteries under 7th Bde.H.Q. for disciplines & Routine.	
	21st		Only from the 16th inst.	
	22.		1 Gun of the 18th Bty out of action. 57 remounts arrive at NOEUX LES MINES Station.	
	23.		In action usual "strafte".	
	24.		C.O. Conference at D.A.	
	25.		C.O. visits all gun positions, wagon lines + B.A.C.	
	26.		Capt. Edgerton Warburton arrives from D.A.C.	
	27.		Capt. Edgerton Warburton takes command of B.A.C.	
	28.		C.O. to Conference at 18th Bty near C.O. to command heavy Group. C.O. temp. transferred to 5th Div. Bde. H.Q. Lieut. L.B. Tansley transferred to 7th Bde. H.Q.	

1577 Wt.W10791/1773 500,000 1/15 D.D.&L. A.D.S.S./Forms/C. 2118.

Army Form C. 2118.

WAR DIARY
or
INTELLIGENCE SUMMARY.
(Erase heading not required.)

Instructions regarding War Diaries and Intelligence Summaries are contained in F. S. Regs., Part II. and the Staff Manual respectively. Title pages will be prepared in manuscript.

Place	Date	Hour	Summary of Events and Information	Remarks and references to Appendices
SAILLY LA BOURSE	29" 30" 31"		C O visits heavy Gun positions and OP's and 'Stuffer' and retaliation fire.	

M Peake
Lt Col.
Commanding 70/RFA
7th

47

1/1 London Bde R.F.a

Jan

Vol XI

Army Form C. 2118.

WAR DIARY
or
INTELLIGENCE SUMMARY.
(Erase heading not required.)

Instructions regarding War Diaries and Intelligence Summaries are contained in F. S. Regs., Part II. and the Staff Manual respectively. Title pages will be prepared in manuscript.

Place	Date	Hour	Summary of Events and Information	Remarks and references to Appendices
SAILLY-LA-BOURSE	Jany 4/5		Lt Ullman & Lt Kimber and 3 N.C.O's to 47th DA Course at GOSNAY.	
	5		C.O. to LES BREBIS with Brigade Major to reconnoitre new position. O.O. to KNOEU & LETI - MINES to Brigade Wagon lines -	
LES BREBIS	6		Section of batteries to new posr at GRENAY.	
	7		C.O and HQ. to LES BREBIS also remaining section of Batteries - B.A.C. to HOUCHIN. Battery wagon lines at BRAQUEMONT. Colonel Batterns Assistant took over front at Sohain	
	8		Registration	
	9		Dr Davison of 14th Bty killed in GRENAY, taking ammunition to gun position	
	10		C.R.A. returned from Sick leave. Lt Col Mackey took command of Group.	
	11		March Back Office -	
	12		C.O. & Adjt to wagon lines -	
	13		Adjt to NOEUX LES MINES to Anti-Aircraft remounts	
	14.		Lt Tuson posted to 19th -	
	15		Capt Lloyd & Lt Swinnerton on leave. Lt Dodgson Adjt Lt Young 2O Capt Ford attached 6.20th. Capt Lloyd att 19th Lt Dodgson posted to 18th Reserve Arty. H.Q.	

1577 Wt.W10791/1773 500,000 1/15 D. D. & L. A.D.S.S./Forms/C. 2118.

Army Form C. 2118.

WAR DIARY
or
INTELLIGENCE SUMMARY.
(Erase heading not required.)

Instructions regarding War Diaries and Intelligence Summaries are contained in F. S. Regs., Part II. and the Staff Manual respectively. Title pages will be prepared in manuscript.

Place	Date	Hour	Summary of Events and Information	Remarks and references to Appendices
LES BREBIS	15	-	2/Lt Tawney posted to H.Q.	
	16	-	2/Lt RA Contin rejoined from 1st Army Artillery School.	
			General Wray on leave - to FR over GRENAY Pat Murknight.	
	18	-	In co-operation with Infantry. 13, 14, 15, 19, 20 shelled enemy working parties.	
	19		Bg DM men tested COISE Y CRASSIER barrages.	
	20		2/Lt HODGKINSON joined from England - posted to B.A.C.	
	21		14, 15, 19, 20 Btees - shelled Cité St Pierre and road junctions.	
	22		Retaliation for heavy shelling of MARDC.	
	23		Major Marshall went to 1st Army Artillery School at AIRE.	
	25		Sgt Belcher to 1st Army Artillery School at LIETTRES.	
			Signalling Course at Div. Arty. Batteries heavily shelling, 2 guns of 13" Bty out of action. 2 guns of 20" sent to 13".	
	26		Heavy bombardment of Trenches and MARDC, especially O.P's.	
			Two guns of 9 Ko. Bty sent up to 20" Bty.	
	27		KAISER'S BIRTHDAY. Bombardment of trenches N of DOUBLE CRASSIER - retaliation all day.	
			More in town - gas shells used - quietened down in evening.	

Army Form C. 2118.

WAR DIARY
or
INTELLIGENCE SUMMARY.
(Erase heading not required.)

Instructions regarding War Diaries and Intelligence Summaries are contained in F. S. Regs., Part II. and the Staff Manual respectively. Title pages will be prepared in manuscript.

Place	Date	Hour	Summary of Events and Information	Remarks and references to Appendices
LES BAEFUR	28		CRA returned from leave. Lt-Col. Massey took over the group.	
			Capt Paine 61st Div Hdq attached to 20th for instruction	
	30		CO. went round wagon lines & B.A.C. Lt Tansley attached 618 Bg.	
			Lt Smigan + Lt Twoon + 3 N.C.Os to 47 Dn Comm of Gosary.	
	31.		Capt Paine 61st Division returned to England —	

Signed [illegible]
Lieut R.Don
for OC 7 to 13d Bde

47

1/y London Bde R.F.A.

Feb

Vol XII

Army Form C. 2118.

WAR DIARY
or
INTELLIGENCE SUMMARY
(Erase heading not required.)

Instructions regarding War Diaries and Intelligence Summaries are contained in F. S. Regs., Part II. and the Staff Manual respectively. Title pages will be prepared in manuscript.

Place	Date	Hour	Summary of Events and Information	Remarks and references to Appendices
LES BREBIS	1		Col. Peal took over command of Group - General Wray being on leave 9 (C) Army C.R.A	
	2		2Lt. Landes rejoined H.Q. Major Lord Gorell went on leave	
	3		Killed enemy shooting parties at a trench junction. N.C.O. went to signalling course to HINGES	
	4		New edition of maps taken into use - Hospital [?] batteries shelled trench junction.	
	5		Major Marshall + Lt. Piley on leave. Assembly trenches Sgt Dorlie Grassier and E of COPSE fired upon - extensive new work for German trenches observed -	
	6		Lt. Dodgson on leave - Lt. Turnbull 5th Lon RMB adjt of Group fired on New German front line and working parties.	
	7		Capt Warburton attached to 18th Battery - 1 Sgt Major + 6 gunners exchanged with DAC for instruction -	
	8		6 gns exchanged with D.A.C. for instruction. 19th fired on trench junction 140 rounds	
	9		Lt Ballantyne + Lt. Mortlemen joined from England. Snipe gun of 19th fired on and damaged entrance to tunnel under CHASSER -	
	10		Shelled trench junctions. N of PUITS 16	

Army Form C. 2118.

WAR DIARY
or
INTELLIGENCE SUMMARY.
(Erase heading not required.)

Instructions regarding War Diaries and Intelligence Summaries are contained in F. S. Regs, Part II. and the Staff Manual respectively. Title pages will be prepared in manuscript.

Place	Date	Hour	Summary of Events and Information	Remarks and references to Appendices
LES BREBIS	11		Fired on working parties - S¹ Pierre & Posts 11	
	12		do and road junction.	
	13		Lt Simmons + 20 men returned from DA course. Three fractise garrisons in morning and 2 in evening - 19ᵗʰ fired with aeroplane observation on Cross Roads M.17.b.	
	14		Mine sprung by enemy near the COPSE. Barrage opened successfully. Major Lord Goll to Course at AIRE - fired on Posts 16 and working parties.	
	15		" Assaulted trenches of FOSSE 11	
	16		Sections of Battalion relieved by 1ˢᵗ DA to Noyelles mines NOEUX-LES-MINES	
	17	5.0 p.m.	Orders to march to rest billets in MAZINGARBE - MINES Cancelled	
		8.0 p.m	Orders received to join Poole Group - attached 1ˢᵗ Division - ???	
			C.O. + R.C's to reconnoitre new position - 39ᵗʰ Bde, Col MacNaughton and 23ʳᵈ Bde Col Hinton took over at mid-day. OO Headquarters to SAUCHOY FARM	
MAZINGARBE	17		MAZINGARBE - 2ⁿᵈ Section of Battn relieved - Battalion complete took up new positions 18ᵗʰ & 19ᵗʰ in FOSSE 7 & 20ᵗʰ in VERMELLES. taking over from 2ⁿᵈ ln Inf Bde Col MacDowell —	

Army Form C.° 2118.

WAR DIARY
or
INTELLIGENCE SUMMARY.
(Erase heading not required.)

Place	Date	Hour	Summary of Events and Information	Remarks and references to Appendices
MAZINGARBE	18		Bties registering -	
	19		draft of 114 men joined -	
	20		9 NCO's & men to signalling coon HQ 4th Corps	
	21	11.0 am	Report of German counter received that Germans wired bombard and attack in afternoon.	
		2.0 pm	Heavy bombardment heard in trench area - FOSSE 7 & GRENAY heavily shelled - Poole Group associates in trench bombardment on German batteries	
	22		Observation impossible owing to snow.	
	23		2/Lt Ballantyne Shuttleworth taken on strength of Brigade	
	25	7 pm	2nd army Spring manoeuvres HERTS Crater - 18/19 Bties opened a barrage - CO & Col Poole reconnoitred trenches in GRENAY	
	26		Orders received for Bde to be relieved by 5 London TAL on 3.4th march -	
	27		Marzingarbe shelled -	
	28		New telephone line from HQ to GRENAY completed.	
	29		operation order for relief cancelled - meeting of BC's in evening. FOSSE 7 heavily shelled - CO & BC's to meet Gen Sanders CRA 2nd DA to reconnoitre new positions	

J.H. Hodgson

47th   5-6

1/2 y London Bde R F a

Vol XIII

Army Form C. 2118.

WAR DIARY
or
INTELLIGENCE SUMMARY.
(Erase heading not required.)

Instructions regarding War Diaries and Intelligence Summaries are contained in F. S. Regs., Part II. and the Staff Manual respectively. Title pages will be prepared in manuscript.

Place	Date	Hour	Summary of Events and Information	Remarks and references to Appendices
	March			
CAMBLAIN	12		Lt. T.G. Folingsby to French Mortar course at St Venant.	
CHATELAIN	13		Inspection of Horses by G.O.C.R.A. Distribution of machine guns by G.O.C. 1st Army. A 19th Ln. Bdy D.C.M. Q.M.S. Paggard	
	14		Officers ride inspected by G.O.C.R.A.	
	15		C.O. & B.C.s to reconnoitre new positions.	
	16		Inspection of horses by D.D.R. 1st Army	
	17		First section of batteries move into action on the CARENCY Sector.	
	18		C.O. to 18th Wagon line to Bois OLHAIN. Adjt to H.Q. 102 Bde Bois Bouvigny. B.A.C. to GAUCHIN LEGAL.	
Bois de Bouvigny	19		Took over at 10.0 am from 102 Bde 23rd Division. 2nd Section Btries moved into action. Group consists of 7th Bde and 2, Cdn How Bty.	
X.2.b.5.5. Chap. Skel 36c SE 1/20,000	20		Registration. C.O. to battery position	
	21		C.O. to Conference at 47 D.A.	
	22		Capt. Sterling 8. 2/2 London 156 R.F.A. attached 19th Bty. C.O. & Brigade Major to O.P.	
	23		Lt. O'Malley 47 D.A.C. attd to 20th Bty. Bin Mtg: working party under Lt Edwards for trench to O.P.	
	24		Heavy fall of snow. B.S.M. Paley & Lot..n for discharge. Working party as above.	
	26		C.O. visits Wagon Lines. Working party for O.P. taken on by 7th Bde only.	

Army Form C. 2118.

WAR DIARY
or
INTELLIGENCE SUMMARY.
(Erase heading not required.)

Instructions regarding War Diaries and Intelligence Summaries are contained in F. S. Regs., Part II. and the Staff Manual respectively. Title pages will be prepared in manuscript.

Place	Date	Hour	Summary of Events and Information	Remarks and references to Appendices
Bois de Bouvigny.	March 28		draft of 23 men received - Conference in Group HQ of B.C's and officers of R.F.C.	
	30		Flammenwerfer demonstration. C.O. and O.O. reconnoitre reserve positions. 212 Battery registration with aeroplane. M.G.R.A. 1st Army to inspect batteries. He expressed satisfaction - Heavies sharp 7am.	
	31.		C.O. to Battalion HQ. One gun of 31st Bty placed at disposal of 46th Div. 212 Bty airplane registration	

M.M. Dodson Lt
Col. London Bde R.F.A.

237 Brigade R.F.A.
237 Bde R.F.A.
Wk 17 hrs 10 pm

WAR DIARY
INTELLIGENCE SUMMARY
(Erase heading not required.)

Instructions regarding War Diaries and Intelligence Summaries are contained in F.S. Regs., Part II. and the Staff Manual respectively. Title pages will be prepared in manuscript.

Army Form C. 2118.

Place	Date	Hour	Summary of Events and Information	Remarks and references to Appendices
BOIS de BOUVIGNY	April 1.		B.G.R.A. visited H.Q. Col Ely took over command ? group. Col Peel on leave	
	2		21st Bty aeroplane registration	
	3		18th Bty aeroplane registration	
	4		Horse inspection by DDR of B.A.C. horses. R.F.C. Observers left HQ	
	6		15th Bty aeroplane registration. Hun aeroplane shot down by our observer	
	7		Telephonists relieved by 8th Bde. 19 & 21st fired on road junction	
			Bdes 15th 19. 21 fired according to Int. programme on Givenchy	
	8	3:25 pm	Same as day before	
	9		All batteries fired on German battery	
			Bombardment of PIMPLE postponed	
	10		Bombardment of PIMPLE. Enemy attack with smoke by 23rd Div.	
			Our aid down by ½	
TREVILLERS	12		Moved Bde HQ from action to Trevillers - Guns stopped from 18 nwt	
	13		CO visited BOUVIGNY	
	14		CO visited major luea	
	17		Corps Commander below	

Army Form C. 2118.

WAR DIARY
or
INTELLIGENCE SUMMARY.
(Erase heading not required.)

Instructions regarding War Diaries and Intelligence Summaries are contained in F.S. Regs., Part II. and the Staff Manual respectively. Title pages will be prepared in manuscript.

Place	Date	Hour	Summary of Events and Information	Remarks and references to Appendices
April			LEFT	
Bo 18 da	18		Moved to Mont. Took over from Captn. E. Rev. Wilkinson C.E. attached	
BOUVIGNY	19	3.30	Rest. Field etc joined HQ. Knet as Adjutant. B Battery transferred to 18 London Battery.	
			29 recruits arrived for Battle.	
	20.		New Battery B/17 Inclindale desired. first B.T.B.A. Temps renewed with 47 SBC.	
	21.		(About) visited New Battery position, hitherto in gun groups. Sermons.	
	22		After all day & several batteries were heavily shelled.	
			Rain. Reinf. reinforcements received from B to 25 London Battery	
	23		Sunday. Service by Rev. Wilkinson in words. German active with rifle fire.	
	24		German Pencel Aircraft very active - R Battery officers visited Bomb HQ.	
	25		7 9 cm on leopard H.R./Battery at DAC. Started 7 cc Germans opened vigorous bombardment	
			on right of our front. All fresh as an front. Our battery fired for an hour.	
	26.		Sea of sand. Bombardment at 3am. 20 & 30 Bligh fired. Confirm of B/s at	
			Group HQ. interrupted by big bombardment by the Germans - mini in center of	
			you & extreme gun & Buffy (in	
	27		Rest. Turkey went into tonight Painephistick. Germans active with R/Battery	
	28.		19 London Battery relieved by R Battery. 192 O. went to ALBERT. Braunfields	

WAR DIARY
or
INTELLIGENCE SUMMARY.
(Erase heading not required.)

Army Form C. 2118.

Place	Date	Hour	Summary of Events and Information	Remarks and references to Appendices
Bois de Bouvigny	April 28		Visited 1st & 90th Bde. B/S stabs at 7.35 pm. Attack on 26th Div front was at Lieple and on 26th front. No Germans got into our front lines.	
	29		Rd 20 L Battn relieved by 12 + 34/5 Ldn R.B. Adv. Park. 1/110 to Comly	
	30		Handed over to Lt Col: Marry at 7.00 pm. Staff in huts. 1/1 Co for Sig moved to DA lines at DAC. Remainder of HQ to be cont'd	
	May 1 2 3		Col: Hall DAC visited HQ. Captain Wood now Major. Count of horses & mules lost at DAC. If it happens etc... Ap Rds & mules 1709 X Polly with to line	

B Smith
Lt & adjt
for OC 237 ∧ de Rka.

47

237 Bde RFA
7 London Bde RFA

Army Form C. 2118.

WAR DIARY
of 237 Bde 7 London Bde RFA

INTELLIGENCE SUMMARY.

(Erase heading not required.)

Instructions regarding War Diaries and Intelligence Summaries are contained in F.S. Regs., Part II. and the Staff Manual respectively. Title pages will be prepared in manuscript.

Place	Date	Hour	Summary of Events and Information	Remarks and references to Appendices
Le Conte	May 1	—	Lt Burgess (20 Blk) evacuated to Rouen.	
"	May 2		Cont. of Enquiry on certain B.A.C. rendus.	
"	May 3		Adjutant visited 47 D.A. & 237 Bty — RSM Cresswell posted to Red HQrs	
"	May 4		C.O. visited 19th Bty at Marat	
"	5		HQ & Bttys skeleton specially drawn. CO. went to DA. Interpreter Gerber arrives	
"	6		Skeleton Drill orderly Bde inter-communicn of DSRA. Lt Burgess to Bty Cadets	
"	7		Church Parade	
"	9		CO. & Adjutant visits 13 Bde RFA, Special positions 247 DA.	
"	10		CO to B.A.C.	
"	11		HQ & Batteries Scheme "in sketch order with Riflemen. CO. visits BAC. Bus Despatched	Gennefeur
"	12		Capt. Capt. went through villages. Field Officers visits D.A. in afternoon	
"	13		Orderly Officers went to new Weymouth & finds Weymouth 47 Bde & 2 D.A.	
"	14		Remains as 237 Bde RFA	
"	15		Changing of horses between 1 Bty & 7 BAC	
"	16		CO, Adjt went to RJ Comp. morphine — also DA	
"	17		Inspection in Marching Order by GOC (Gen Cuthbert)	

WAR DIARY
or
INTELLIGENCE SUMMARY.

Army Form C. 2118.

Place	Date	Hour	Summary of Events and Information	Remarks and references to Appendices
Le Coife	May 18-19	—	Co. visits base rehearses phases of advance - Advance paths to W.Ls & Major X night ops. Co. to sea on S.S. [Emperatine].	
Boesele Hay	20	—	Took over Rt Group from Col Sky.	
	21	6.30am	Minenwerfers began early in morning. Rt Group retaliated. General artly activity.	
		3.30pm	Beavey mid 5th before & much shelling (with grenades also) of all front posts. Balkan shelled - Steady barrage till 9. or pm - On battline retaliates. Portland Sutton remains in hands of Col Dulle. Camellia & the 15th - Sgt Cook wounded. Quelwalle killed - Jltd Sgt Slestiew wounded.	
	22	2.30am	Col Lawe came up & took over command of Rt Group. German reports as having taken our front & support lines and reete.	
BERTHONVAL	23	2.0pm	Transfers Bde HQ to Bertenval and took over Bethonval Group consisting of A.B. & C /137 A/112 & C/113 Bttys - No further fighting that night. Steady rate of fire varying from 100 rounds per bty per hour downwards, on German positions - 4 & 15 L took of their positions in the same alignants requested - Col 7.35 inclusive per hour our battline & terrific attack on ground lost on May 21.	

WAR DIARY
or
INTELLIGENCE SUMMARY.
(Erase heading not required.)

Place	Date	Hour	Summary of Events and Information	Remarks and references to Appendices
Bethonval	May 24		Quiet day. Steady rate of fire kept up. On HQ shells with 8.2" hows. No major casualties. Col Bulla went round trenches returning from afternoon's bombing posts, trenches etc.	
	25		Captains Temple & Campbell of C/113 & A/112 visited trenches before. Shelling much less than before. Slight knock of enemy shrapnel at Zouave Valley.	
	26		Howks went to 41st Bde A/113 at 11 a.m. 20th & 18th how's during the evening. Also A/112 & C/113. 19th B/15 to the HQ left in the evening — 19 Bty & Wagon lines. HQ marched to BRIAS arriving 5.30 am ap 27	
BRIAS	27		19th Ldn B/15 arrived in the afternoon. Billets themselves good, cooking poor.	
	28		C.O. & adjutant to D.A.	
	29		HQ & 19th & B/15 marched to Burbi - billets thick in arms. 18 & 20th Bdes waiting orders	
	30		to march	
	31			

[signature]
for OC 7 Bde RHA

WAR DIARY
or
INTELLIGENCE SUMMARY.
(Erase heading not required.)

Army Form C. 2118.

234 Sec RE 47
16

Place	Date	Hour	Summary of Events and Information	Remarks and references to Appendices
BARLIN	June 2		Inspection of lines of B/237 and Bde HQrs by DSO/S XARVS.	
"	3		Captain H.C. Morgan arrived from 3/1 London Bde. attached to B/237 Btty.	
	5		Adj: visited A/237 C/237 at Bertrancourt in adm. 2/Lt Hopkinson left for a T.M. course at Mony.	
	7		Adj: visited A/237 C/237 Mayor Lucie at Cau Ham L'Abbé.	
	10		Adj: Started visiting Sonchez Group HQ & going over wires preparatory to taking over of the Group by 236 Bde HQ (RT Group) to whom Adj: & 6 telephonists was lent.	
	11		ditto. 13th. ditto. 15th. ditto.	
	12			
	14 / 15		A/237 & B/237 Came out of action. Remained overnight at Noir Wagon huis coming under these HQrs from 6 p.m.	
			Section of A.B.T.C./237 moved into action in the Right Group — Souchez sector.	
			under Tactical command of Lt. Col. Lowe.	
	16		Adj: & 6 signallers went to RT Group HQ.	
	17		Aeroplane & artillery activity apparent. 2/Lt Ballantyne went on leave.	
	20		Took wing remount from Dép. for the Brigade.	
	21		Lt Kimber & 2/Lt Flingoby wounded in Souchez II.	

WAR DIARY
or
INTELLIGENCE SUMMARY.
(Erase heading not required.)

Army Form C. 2118.

Place	Date	Hour	Summary of Events and Information	Remarks and references to Appendices
BARLIN	22		Lt Kniker died of wounds at Barlin. 2/Lt Flugoly died of wounds at Aix-Noulette.	
	23		Adj: attached to C/237. 2/Lt Flugoly buried at Aix Noulette 7 P.M. by Rev. Wilkinson.	
	24		Lt Kniker buried at Barlin by Rev. Wilkinson. Artillery activity on our front.	
	25		2 guns (van Att (237) to J.O.M. Artillery activity continues.	
	27		C.O. reconnoitred positions and OPs for BAJOLLE LINE. Artillery activity as before.	
			Adj: returned to Bde HQ. Raid on German Trenches in Angres Secta. "	
			in which A & B/237 cut wire & C/237 also took part.	
	28		C.O. reconnoitred BAJOLLE LINE.	
	29		Gun of A/237 K.I.O.M.	
	30		Adj: visited wagon lines of A.B.C/237 & A/236 & D/236.	

P.H. Pilditch Lt
(London)
Adj. for O.C. 237/Brigade R.F.A.

47th Divisional Artillery

237th BRIGADE

ROYAL FIELD ARTILLERY.

JULY 1916

Army Form C. 2118.

WAR DIARY
or
INTELLIGENCE SUMMARY.
(Erase heading not required.)

237th BRIGADE R.F.A.

Vol 17

Place	Date	Hour	Summary of Events and Information	Remarks and references to Appendices
BARLIN	July 1st		Horses of A, B & C 237th Bde inspected by D.D.V.S. Colonel and Adjutant went to Wagon lines	
	2nd		C.O. to Right Group in the enemy.	
	3rd		C.O. acted as liaison officer with 140th Infy. Brigade Commander for raid on Right Battalion front, staying in line for night.	
	4th		C.O. returned from line. Adjt round Wagon lines.	
	5th		Adjt & R.S.M. to Right Group.	
	6th		C.O. and Adjt to Right Group. Taking over of Groups postponed.	
	7th		Adjt to Right Group Wagon lines to arrange for take over.	
	8th		C.O. and Adjt to Wagon lines in morning. Batteries took part in raid during night - gas being used. (Burst of Groups on A,B,C; D 236; A,B,C, 237; B223) 9TH bty. Brigade took over Command of RIGHT GROUP with Wagon lines at	
AIX-NOULETTE	9th		BOYEFFLES. 2nd Lieut Bukpoi (236th Bde) attacked as signal officer. Carried out stafe on roads behind enemy lines.	
	10th		Colonel Allen and Adjt of 316th Bde R.N. Division attached with part of H.Q. Staff for instruction. To A,B 237 and C 236.Ria B, A & C Batteries	

Army Form C. 2118.

WAR DIARY
or
INTELLIGENCE SUMMARY. 237th BRIGADE R.F.A.

(Erase heading not required.)

Place	Date	Hour	Summary of Events and Information	Remarks and references to Appendices
AIX-NOULETTE	July 10th			
	11th		316 Bde have 3 officers and 30 men attached respectively. Colonel & Adjt attend conference with BGRA at Infantry Bde HQ. Orderly Officer with Staff Capt. 47 DA & DTMO visit all Tauer Mortar Blics & Batteries.	
	12th		BC.s reconnoitre sniper gun positions. C.O. with Orderly Officer, Colonel Allen and his Bight to 4 Trench Mortars Battery and H.R. Right & Left Battalions. Minenwerfers active taken in day on Left Batta. we retaliated with Ballews & T.M.S. All observers make reports to Division on 2"Line Enemy wire & defences.	
	13th		Conference at Groups H.Q. with Bde Major 47 DA. Trench mortars were cutting all day covered by 18 pdr. Blics or O.P.s & trellis, roads. 10 recruits taken over from D.A.C.	
	14th		CO. to Left Batta H.Q. Trench mortars entrench on Salient in M32D. maplework covered by 18 pdr. Batteries, which also cut wire registration. Orderly Officer of 316 attached for instruction as Signal Officer. Nine officers from D.A.C. and Brigades attached to A236 for instruction.	

Army Form C. 2118.

WAR DIARY
or
INTELLIGENCE SUMMARY. 237th BRIGADE R.F.A.

(Erase heading not required.)

Place	Date	Hour	Summary of Events and Information	Remarks and references to Appendices
AIX-NOULETTE	July 15th		Colonel Gemmell, his Adjt and Orderly Officers and some signallers attached to Group HQ. to takeover eventually. 3 officers and 30 men form each of A.B. & C. Btys of his Bde. (225 Bde.) attached to A,B & C 237 respectively. 18 p.m. Batteries were-ranking, and much retaliation to our message. T.M.s also bombarded.	
	16th		Colonel attends conference of G.O.C. Division at 141 Inf. Bde. HQ. C.O. to Infantry Battalions. 6" Battery bombarded area of raid. Colonel Lowe (236th Bde.) as liaison to 141st Infantry Brigade. Raid proceeded from 11.30 p.m. to 7 a.m. (17th). Barrage never cut by RIGHT GROUP, two batteries LEFT GROUP, Trench mortars, Stokes mortars and 60 pans on Salient in M32D preparing to 141st Inf. Bde. raid.	
	17th		Adjt to LORETTE. Enemy very active with heavy trench mortars during early evening. GROUP retaliated vigorously with 18pdrs, 4.5 Hows & T.M.s. C3/6 Bty attached men charged to B236 Bty.	
	18th		Adjt to Y and Z Trench Mortar Bttes. C.O. to Batteries. GROUP Poisoned Gas minor operation at 2 am (19th) on Salient in M32D, bombarding cut minor operation at 2 am (19th) on Salient in M32D, bombarding	

Army Form C. 2118.

WAR DIARY
or
INTELLIGENCE SUMMARY. 237th BRIGADE R.F.A.
(Erase heading not required.)

Place	Date	Hour	Summary of Events and Information	Remarks and references to Appendices
AIX-NOULETTE	July 19th		For few minutes before small raid.	
	20th		Duel by Trench Mortars. C.O. and Adjt. to O.P.'s in evening. C.O. to R.N. Dragoon Infantry Bde. Colonel Gemmell Orderly Officer now attached to H.Q. Telephone exchange changed over.	
	21st		Officers attached to A236 went back to units. A236 Bty (one section) reinforces new position dugouts. Adjt. & Orderly Officer to Batteries.	
	22nd		Colonel Gemmell with Orderly Officer to BERTHONVAL Battery (B236). Bombardment of M32D salient by Trench Mortars afternoon — no retaliation.	
	23rd		C.O. visits Battalions and Liaison Officers. Section 75pdr. Battery came in forward position. Trench Mortars trieden enemy approaches.	
	24th 25th		Section of 15pdr. Battery put into forward position. C.R.A. visits O.P.'s. Both Howitzer Batteries transferred from GROUP. All H.Q. Staff sent away except NCO's requisite. Battery.	
	26th		Battery Naponleur moved to MAREST with H.Q. Napoleur, Extract, all limbers at COUPIGNY.	

Army Form C. 2118.

WAR DIARY
or
INTELLIGENCE SUMMARY.
(Erase heading not required.)

237th BRIGADE RFA

Places	Date	Hour	Summary of Events and Information	Remarks and references to Appendices
AIX-NOULETTE	July 27th		C.O. to forward positions in evening. 18 pdr. Batteries carried out systematic bombardment of hostile support and near trenches in Souchez section at three periods during the night.	
	28th		MGRA Corps, CRA 63rd Division and CRA 47th Division to Group HQ and Bty Co gun positions in morning. Orderly Officer of the remainder of Brigade visited hostile support and near trenches. 18 pdr. Batteries carried out bombardment of hostile support and near trenches at 3 periods during the night.	
GRICOURT	29th		C.O. Adjt and Office staff with BCs and details of Batteries travelled by motor lorries to rest Trench Mortar Battery to rest at MAREST and GRICOURT with Trench Mortar Battery to rest at MONCHEZ.	
	30th	4:30 a.m. 5:30 a.m.	Brigade Galloping officers started and met Staff Captain at MONCHEZ. Battery Galloping parties to MONCHEZ. Brigade marched to Gillets	
MONCHEZ	31st		at MONCHEZ arriving 3/am. Officers from each Battery & HQ to inspect new gun at FREVENT. Demonstration by Armament Artificers of laying down of Buffer.	

Signature

1577 Wt. W10791/1773 500,000 1/15 D.D. & L. A.D.S.S./Forms/C. 2118.

47th Divisional Artillery.

237th BRIGADE

ROYAL FIELD ARTILLERY.

AUGUST 1 9 1 6

Army Form C. 2118.

VR 18

WAR DIARY
INTELLIGENCE SUMMARY

of 237th Brigade R.F.A.(?)
August 1916

(Erase heading not required.)

Instructions regarding War Diaries and Intelligence Summaries are contained in F.S. Regs., Part II. and the Staff Manual respectively. Title pages will be prepared in manuscript.

Place	Date	Hour	Summary of Events and Information	Remarks and references to Appendices
	Aug.			
MAVANS	1st	9 A.M.	Myself and Intelligence Officer went to Mondicourt	
		7 P.M.	Brigade marched into MAVANS from MONCHEZ billets.	
	2nd		5 reinforcements (O.R.) rejoined from Base.	
	3rd	-	Visit by B.G.R.A. 2/Lt Culbert O.C. Z T.M. Battery evacuated. Gnr. Farmer and Dr. Sweeney (H.Q.) evacuated. 2/Lt Ayers reports from Base.	
	4th		Brigade and Battery staffs on drill order.	
LE PONCHEZ	5th	4 A.M.	Brigade and Battery Billeting Parties at LE PONCHEZ	
		7 A.M.	Brigade marched into billets at LE PONCHEZ. A.D.V.S. meets Brigade in afternoon.	
	6th		Church Parade at Bde. H.Q. French Mortar Batteries inspected by B.G.R.A.	
	7th		Drill Order manoeuvres by whole Brigade (including Z T.M. Bty) in conjunction with 238th Brigade R.F.A. under orders of B.G.R.A.	
	8th		Full Order for Brigade H.Q. Staff, and Battery Staffs. Conference of C.O. with B.C.s.	
	9th		Divisional Artillery Field Day Scheme near BOUFFLERS	
LANCHES	10th	9.30 A.M.	Brigade and Battery Billeting Parties meet Staff Capt. & Div. Arty. & all sub billets in LANCHES	

Army Form C. 2118.

WAR DIARY
or
INTELLIGENCE SUMMARY.
(Erase heading not required.)

Instructions regarding War Diaries and Intelligence Summaries are contained in F. S. Regs., Part II. and the Staff Manual respectively. Title pages will be prepared in manuscript.

Place	Date	Hour	Summary of Events and Information	Remarks and references to Appendices
LANCHES	Aug. 10th (Cont)	11 A.M.	Brigade marched into billets at LANCHES. B.G.R.A. visits Brigade.	
NAOURS	11th	9 A.M.	Brigade Billeting Officer and Billeting Parties met Staff Capt. 47th Div. Orly. at HAVERNAS and were allotted billets in NAOURS	
		10.30 A.M.	Brigade marched into billets at NAOURS	
		2 P.M.	Brigade Billeting Officer with Staff Capt. 47th Div Orly to allot billets at BÉHENCOURT	
		5 P.M.	Billeting Parties arrive at BÉHENCOURT.	
BÉHENCOURT	12th	6 P.M.	Brigade marched into BÉHENCOURT. Aytnew B.C.s. go up to the twenty days reconnoitre positions. Conference of C.O. and B.C.s.	
	13th	—	Brigade Orderly Officer and advance Billeting parties to 176th Brigade in letters to take over communications. 2 T.M. Battery moves up to ALBERT 126 D.A.C.	
MAMETZ	14th	—	C.O. arrived to take over line from 176th Brigade with positions North of MAMETZ. Batteries take over by 4 P.M. 2g Reinwards taken over.	
	15th		Much firing by Batteries. New Dugouts by started by Betts & Batteries.	

1577 Wt.W10791/1773 500,000 1/15 D. D. & L. A.D.S.S./Forms/C. 2118.

WAR DIARY or INTELLIGENCE SUMMARY.

Army Form C. 2118.

Place	Date	Hour	Summary of Events and Information	Remarks and references to Appendices
MAMETZ	Aug. 16th	—	Batteries had stages on roads.	
	17th		~~Reconnaissance~~ Operations carried out in conjunction with an attack by the 44th Brigade on Switch Line. 2/Lieuts' Bates (B Battery) and Bowen (C Battery) wounded and 2/Lt Moulman suffering from Shell-Shock.	
	18th		Batteries kept up 3 hours barrage in the afternoon during our attacks. Road shoots during the night. Capt. to O.P. in front line.	
	19th		2nd Lieut Bowen to Field Ambulance. Slow barrage to cover advance in Scotch Line.	
	20.		Fire all day on point in MARTINPUICH. At 5 P.M. Barrage opened. Observing Officers saw enemy attacking at HIGH WOOD. This attack was crumpled up and attackers followed up, destroying rear, by our Battery, Brigade (A Bty). Attacking party consisted of over half a Battalion.	
	21st		Fired in conjunction with Smoke attack by Division on left, more than usual shelling by enemy – 12 "M" shells near Bde Hd Shelters & C Battery. MWM	

1577 Wt.W.10791/1773 500,000 1/15 D. D. & L. A.D.S.S./Forms/C. 2118.

Army Form C. 2118.

WAR DIARY
or
INTELLIGENCE SUMMARY.
(Erase heading not required.)

Place	Date	Hour	Summary of Events and Information	Remarks and references to Appendices
MAMETZ	Aug 22nd	-	Hurricane. 2/Lt. Pallis all arrived from 47" DAC and was posted to B Battery. 2/Lt. Mackie from same unit posted C Battery.	
	23rd	-	2/Lt Mottram evacuated to England. Batteries fired all night on new German trench. Gnr. Bailey killed and Bdr. Richards wounded (both C/B/4)	
	24th	-	C.O. with O.O. to O.P. in front line. C.O. after to Sgt Brigade and Batteries barraged during small attack on reminder of "Intermediate Trench". Sgt Wagner &c killed and Sgt. Major Conway (both A Bty) wounded in front line.	
	25th	-	C.O. to Headquarters 47" DAC.	
	26th	-	Reconnaissance of Headquarters. Very violent bombardment by enemy near Batteries. CO. to Div Arty.	
	27th	-	Gnr Smith (B Bty) wounded by shrapnel.	
	28th	-	Much very heavy artillery fire on German lines.	
	29th	-	2 T.M. Battery moved in the line. Very heavy thunderstorm stops operations.	
	30th	-	CO. to front line in the morning. Barraged enemy forward of Intermediate Trench during day. Belt Forward Bearings.	

Army Form C. 2118.

WAR DIARY
or
INTELLIGENCE SUMMARY.
(Erase heading not required.)

Place	Date	Hour	Summary of Events and Information	Remarks and references to Appendices
MAMETZ	Aug. 30 (cont)	—	Officer post to report to 47th Div Arty that 130 O.R. and 4 officers of enemy surrendered him. Intermediate French. Heavy barrage now Cole pillow valley. 17 & 18 Btys have allied mitrailleuse wood Brigade Major reels B. Bty shells off [illegible] 8" 5.9 & 5" gun rounds.	
	3 pm	—	Bde HQ	

Im Robert
Lieut. Col Colg
237th Bde R.F.A.(T)

237 Bde RFA (T)

Vol 19

WAR DIARY
INTELLIGENCE SUMMARY.

September 1916

Army Form C. 2118.

Place	Date	Hour	Summary of Events and Information	Remarks and references to Appendices
MAMETZ	Sept. 1st		Batteries carried out heavy barrage of hostile roads	
	2nd		Barraged on zone of Division on the Right.	
	3rd		Fired in support of attack on HIGH WOOD	
	5th		Z Trench Mortar Battery went into action before MARTINPUICH	
	6th		2nd Lieut. R.H. WEBB joined Brigade from 47th D.A.C.	
	7th		2nd Lieut. T. BALLANTYNE (B Bty) A Bty personnel to Major Knox — one section from Martin Puich to field Ambulance — Sick. One section under command of O.C. B Bty. One section under command of O.C. C Bty.	
			Fired at all night on German working parties	
	8th		Batteries barraged on attack by 1st Div. on HIGH WOOD	
	12th		Brigade zone changed from Intermediate Trench and MARTINPUICH front to HIGH WOOD	
	13th		Billeted 102 Brigade R.F.A. Abrevaiue run.	
	14th		C.O. to 140 Infantry Brigade as liaison officer for reconnaissance of	

Army Form C. 2118.

WAR DIARY
or
INTELLIGENCE SUMMARY.
(Erase heading not required.)

Place	Date	Hour	Summary of Events and Information	Remarks and references to Appendices
MAMETZ	14th Cont.		Offensive Batteries fired on set. Registration stages. Road for advance (by Batteries reconnoitred by Lieut MORGAN. (B Bty)	
	15th		Barraged for general attack on whole front at 6.20 PM – G.H.Q. barrage tables & no sooner as HIGH WOOD was captured fired on FLERS LINE. Lieuts P.H. DODGSON (A Bty) and R.B. ULLMAN (C Bty) acted as F.O.O's during the attack. A/B Bty made reconnaissance forward and B/Bty went forward to new position at HIGH WOOD at 5 P.M. A Bty went to forward position at HIGH WOOD at 10 P.M.	
HIGH WOOD	16th		Brigade H.Q. moved forward to vacated C Bty position – C Bty assumed B position at HIGH WOOD at 6 P.M. 2nd Lieut LUND fired from 47°D.4°C. 1 man of A Bty fired.	
	17th		Fired for an attack on DROP ALLEY. One man of A Bty wounded.	
	18th		O.C. B Bty to Div Arty H.Q. for two days. Carried out usual heavy barrage. C.O. came back from Liaison duty.	
	19th		2nd Lieut LUND attached to A Bty. 2nd Lieut WEBB (A Bty) and 6 men (A Bty) wounded. Fired on S.O.S. calls during the night	

Army Form C: 2118.

WAR DIARY
or
INTELLIGENCE SUMMARY.
(Erase heading not required.)

Instructions regarding War Diaries and Intelligence Summaries are contained in F. S. Regs., Part II, and the Staff Manual respectively. Title pages will be prepared in manuscript.

Place	Date	Hour	Summary of Events and Information	Remarks and references to Appendices
HIGH WOOD	21st		Batteries very heavily shelled all night with gas shells — LIEUT S.E. PIXLEY C Bty and two men (C & A Btys) gassed.	
	23rd		Barraged FLERS LINE while infantry took two lines BDE to the west of it. Many of A Bty gassed. B Bty personnel now out of line — one section taken over by C Bty — one section taken over by A Bty.	
MAMETZ	23rd		2 men of A Bty wounded. 238th Bgde took over Batteries and H.Q. all personnel coming out to reserve — C Bty to reserve position, A and B Batteries to rest at Neponhes at BÉCOURT WOOD. C Bty position east of MAMETZ WOOD, BDE H.Q. in reserve to supply of guns to DIV. ARTY. near MAMETZ. Adjutant to Divisional Artillery H.Q. for attachment temporarily. D/238 Battery rides Brigade for letters.	
	24th		D/238 Howitzer Bty fired all night on EAUCOURT L'ABBAYE. 2 men of C Bty wounded. D/238 from support of guns attack on repair.	
	26th		D/235 takes over position and guns of D/238 and are under Brigade for letters. Trumpeter PURCHASE (15 Bty) obtains MILITARY MEDAL.	

1577 Wt.W10791/1773 500,000 1/15 D. D. & L. A.D.S.S./Forms/C. 2118.

WAR DIARY
or
INTELLIGENCE SUMMARY.

Army Form C. 2118.

Place	Date	Hour	Summary of Events and Information	Remarks and references to Appendices
MAMETZ	27		2nd Lieut LUND to Field Ambulance with gas poisoning.	

Infield
Lt Col Comdg
237. Brigade R.F.A.(C)

237: Brigade R.F.A.

Army Form C. 2118.

Vol 20

WAR DIARY
or
INTELLIGENCE SUMMARY
(Erase heading not required.)

Place	Date	Hour	Summary of Events and Information	Remarks and references to Appendices
MAMETZ	Oct. 1st		Brigade still in reserve — C/237 (& D/235) Bde attached to C/237 (& D/235) Brigade as Depôt Batteries for Army of the Divisional Artillery. Attack on EAUCOURT L'ABBAYE — 1/50. Brigade did not take part.	
	2nd			
	6th		Adjutant still at H.Q. Divisional Artillery. C.O. went to Infantry Brigade H.Q. with the intention of arranging for the attacks on the Divisional Artilleries between Infantry and the Provisional Artilleries between WARLENCOURT line. OC B/237 Battery in temporary command of Brigade. Bde H.Q. Kapon line moved up to MAMETZ — new Napon line for Batteries reconnoitred. Advance parties to take over positions of 236 Brigade in action.	
	7th			
EAUCOURT L'ABBAYE	8th	4.30 P.M.	Adjutant returned from attachment at Div. Arty. H.Q. at 4.30 P.M. Brigade took over positions and defence of line in BUTTE DE WARLENCOURT sector from 236 Brigade R.F.A. Group consists in action of OC A/237 in command of his Battery and section of B/237; OC C/237 in command of his Battery and section of B/237 and D/236 Howitzers. Battery Batteries behind EAUCOURT L'ABBAYE, Bde H.Q. at HIGH WOOD.	

WAR DIARY
or
INTELLIGENCE SUMMARY.
(Erase heading not required.)

Army Form C. 2118.

Place	Date	Hour	Summary of Events and Information	Remarks and references to Appendices
EAUCOURT L'ABBAYE	Oct 9.		C.O. returned from liaison duties with Infantry Brigade.	
	10.		Section of 40" Howitzer Battery placed in Group with position near A/237 Battery.	
	11.		OC B/237 returned. OC C/237 in action with personnel. OC 50" Bayard RFA, 9" Divisional Artillery with Adjutant attached to Brigade HQ. and two officers and small party tracing Batteries to prepare for relief. Batteries fired during the afternoon in a feint attack.	
	12. 2.5 PM.		Attack on BUTTE DEWARLANCOURT and WARLANCOURT line by 9" Divisional Infantry. 2nd Lieut O'EDWARDS of A/237 acted as F.O.O. cont. OC's A&B/237 also observed. Batteries were fired on barrages during the attack which was not entirely successful. 1 man A/237 badly wounded. 2nd Lieut WEBB and Sergt KERSEY (both A/237) died of wounds in hospital.	
	13.		Batteries relieved at 5 PM. by 9" Divl Artillery and OC 50" Bayard RFA took over command of Group. Brigade marched from Eaucourt starting point at BECOURT, and marched via ALBERT at 10 PM.	

Army Form C. 2118.

WAR DIARY
or
INTELLIGENCE SUMMARY.
(Erase heading not required.)

Instructions regarding War Diaries and Intelligence Summaries are contained in F. S. Regs., Part II. and the Staff Manual respectively. Title pages will be prepared in manuscript.

Place	Date	Hour	Summary of Events and Information	Remarks and references to Appendices
PIERREGOT	Oct 14th	8 A.M.	Brigade arrived at billets at PIERREGOT having marched via LA HOUSSOYE and BEHENCOURT	
	15th		OC B/237 on special leave to England for opening of Parliament.	
AMPLIER	16th	6 A.M.	Brigade marched to billets at AMPLIER arriving at 2 P.M.	
LIGNY-SUR-CANCHE	17th		Brigade marched at 6.30 A.M. via OUTREBOIS (watering) to billets at LIGNY-SUR-CANCHE arriving at 3 P.M.	
HEUCHIN	18th		Marched at 6.0 A.M. via RAMECOURT (watering) and NAVRANS to HEUCHIN arriving at 3 P.M.	
REBECQE	19th		Brigade marched at 7 A.M. to billets at REBECQE arriving at 3 P.M.	
ABEELE	20th		Brigade marched at 4.30 A.M. via HAZEBROUCK and STEEN VOORDE to billeting area near ABEELE (BELGIUM). Advance parties to take over batteries in action at YPRES. Major Lord Gorell OC B/237 awarded the D.S.O.	
	22nd		OO arrived at H.Q. 5th Brigade R.F.A. 2nd Australian Division and	

1577 Wt.W10791/1773 500,000 1/15 D. D. & L. A.D.S.S./Forms/C. 2118.

Army Form C. 2118.

237 Bde R.F.A.

WAR DIARY
or
INTELLIGENCE SUMMARY

(Erase heading not required.)

November 1916

Vol 21

Place	Date	Hour	Summary of Events and Information	Remarks and references to Appendices
YPRES	Nov. 1st		Batteries still in action near SOUTHERN GATE of YPRES, the LEFT GROUP consisting of the Three Batteries of the Brigade with C & D/238 Batteries and 2 Trench Mortar Battery. G.O.C. Division visited Battery positions.	
	Nov. 2nd			
	3rd		C.O. went on leave – Major Lord Gorell (or B/237) temporary Group Commander. Much Trench Mortar activity on the part of the enemy.	
	5th		Reserve positions reconnoitred. Alternative positions reconnoitred.	
	6th			
	7th		Orders issued for the Reorganisation of the Divisional Artillery – in which orders Batteries were to be as follows – sections of A/237 to A and B/235 Batteries; sections of B/237 to 34th and B/238 Batteries and sections of C/237 to C/235 and C/238 Batteries – giving 6 gun batteries. Conference between C.R.A. and O's.C. 237 and 238 Brigades and arranged. By this C/237 Battery gave Right Section to A/237 and Left Section to B/237. Each of which gave one to the Brigade as a	

Army Form C. 2118.

WAR DIARY
or
INTELLIGENCE SUMMARY.

(Erase heading not required.)

Instructions regarding War Diaries and Intelligence Summaries are contained in F. S. Regs., Part II. and the Staff Manual respectively. Title pages will be prepared in manuscript.

Place	Date	Hour	Summary of Events and Information	Remarks and references to Appendices
YPRES	Oct 22 contd.		at 7 P.M. took over command of LEFT GROUP ARTILLERY. Group consists of A,B,C Batteries 237 Brigade and C and D Batteries 235 Brigade. With H.Q. in "Railway Dugouts" south of ZILLEBEKE LAKE	
	25th		Batteries fired while a counterfelt was blown near HILL 60.	
	28th		C/237 pulls reinforced gun.	
	30th		Batteries fired from 2 P.M. to 5 P.M. on organised bombardment of enemy trenches with feint attack. 4 Medium Trench Mortars and one Heavy Trench Mortar now part of Group for tactics.	

~~signature~~
Lt Colonel
Commanding 237 Brigade R.F.A.

Army Form C. 2118.

WAR DIARY
or
INTELLIGENCE SUMMARY

(Erase heading not required.)

Instructions regarding War Diaries and Intelligence Summaries are contained in F. S. Regs., Part II. and the Staff Manual respectively. Title Pages will be prepared in manuscript.

Place	Date	Hour	Summary of Events and Information	Remarks and references to Appendices
YPRES	7 (cont.)		Six gun Battery; A/237 to 235 Bryade, B/237 to 238 Bryade. 2nd Lieut. GOATMAN (A/237) left to 47th DAC. Conference of BCs on Reorganisation details.	
	8th		Group now covering two Battalion front. Communications withdrawn Right Battalion withdrawn. OC A/237 returned from leave.	
	10th		Heavy French Mortar and Minenwerfer bombardment on left Battalion front by the enemy. Batteries retaliated all this afternoon.	
	11th		Forward Brigade Telephone Exchange moved back. Heavy trench mortar activity by enemy – Batteries retaliated. 2nd Lieut Jacques left to 60th Div. from B/237 Bty. One man A Battery killed.	
	12th		GOC Division visited Batteries. Retaliation Scheme "A" for trench mortar.	
	15th		CO. returned from leave.	
	16.		Scheme "A" in conjunction with Heavy Artillery again fired on – very successful. OC C/237 Battery returned from leave. Lieut R. ULLMAN. and 2 Lieut. O. EDWARDS to Hospital Sick.	

Army Form C. 2118.

WAR DIARY
or
INTELLIGENCE SUMMARY
(Erase heading not required.)

Instructions regarding War Diaries and Intelligence Summaries are contained in F.S. Regs., Part II. and the Staff Manual respectively. Title Pages will be prepared in manuscript.

Place	Date	Hour	Summary of Events and Information	Remarks and references to Appendices
YPRES	Nov. 17th		Adjutant went on leave. Retaliation Scheme with Heavy Artillery fired on at 10 P.M. — enemy trenchmortars fire ceased. 2nd Lieut. Macfarlane attached A/237 from 47th D.A.C.	
	19th		Retaliation Scheme again fired on at 4 P.M.	
	21st		Inspection of Battery Wagon Lines by G.O.C. Division. Single towed gun pit on by Groups at ZILLEBEKE.	
	22nd		2nd Lieut MASTJones A/237 Battery attached from 47th D.A.	
	23rd		2 Towed Modes Battery now cutting. Batteries fired on Potsdam. Scheme "C" at 3 P.M. (approx)	
	24th		Scheme "C" as retaliation for trench mortarfire again fired at 2.30 P.M. Reorganisation of the administration of the Batteries started on.	
	25th		2nd Lieut HAMBOHN rejoined from ENGLAND. A/237 exchanged with RIGHT GROUP to 34th Battery which took over its position and gone. A/237 takes up 34th Battery position.	

2449 Wt. W14957/M90 750,000 1/16 J.B.C. & A. Forms/C.2118/12.

Army Form C. 2118.

WAR DIARY
or
INTELLIGENCE SUMMARY
(Erase heading not required.)

Place	Date	Hour	Summary of Events and Information	Remarks and references to Appendices
YPRES	27th	12 midnight	A/237 & Battery plus Right Section C/237 became new C/235 Battery. B/237 Battery plus Left Section C/237 became new C/238 Battery. Sections all remaining (actually) as before postings. All surplus personnel posted 47th Div Arty. Details and temporarily attached to Ballincur — Brigade H.Q. attached new C/238 Battery until relief of Group H.Q.	
	29		Adjutant to hospital sick (in ENGLAND). No Trench Mortar firing by the Group for 4 days except in retaliation for enemy messages activity.	

[signature]
Lieut. Col.
Command 237th Bgde. R.F.A.

www.ingramcontent.com/pod-product-compliance
Lightning Source LLC
Chambersburg PA
CBHW081554160426
43191CB00011B/1931